Understanding and Accepting Anxiety

Learn How to Manage Anxiety and Have Successful Relationships

Table of Contents

Introduction

Anxiety stands as a formidable thread that weaves its way through the complexities of our minds, often disrupting the very fabric of our social connections. This is especially true in the busy world and whirlwind of modern life. With this book, the main idea is to begin a journey that gives us the tools to unravel the complexities of this omnipresent emotional state, shedding light on its impact on relationships and the human experience.

Anxiety, a term often thrown casually into conversation, encompasses a spectrum of emotions that can be both elusive and overwhelming. From the subtle hints of worry to the paralyzing grip of panic, its manifestations are diverse and can profoundly affect the way we relate to the world around us. As we delve deeper into the pages of this book, we navigate through the nuances of anxiety, deciphering its symptoms that often linger beneath the surface, subtly influencing our thoughts, actions, and interpersonal dynamics.

Reflecting on the limitations that anxiety imposes on social interaction reveals the intricate dance between self and other. Fear of judgment, constant anticipation of the worst-case scenario, and perpetual worry about one's own adequacy hinder the flow of genuine connection. This exploration aims to not only illuminate the complexities of anxiety but also serve as a bridge to empathetic understanding, fostering compassion for those who struggle with this intricate emotional terrain.

This deep sense of fear, like dread and unease, is part of the human experience and often serves as a natural response to stressors. While a temporary state of anxiety can be adaptive and provide a boost of energy and focus to meet challenges, anxiety disorders are characterized by persistent, overwhelming fear.

The origins of anxiety disorders are complex and involve factors such as genetics, brain biology, chemistry, stress, and environmental influences. Certain personality traits, traumatic experiences, family history of mental disorders, and specific physical health conditions also contribute to risk (MedlinePlus, 2023).

We will see that the symptoms of anxiety, whether subtle or overt, manifest in countless ways: racing thoughts, restlessness, muscle tension, and an ever-present feeling of restlessness. These symptoms not only permeate our internal landscapes but also overshadow our social interactions. It is crucial to recognize the challenges people face in forging and maintaining meaningful connections, especially understanding the limits that anxiety imposes on social interactions and that it can influence our workplace experience.

Symptoms of anxiety disorders encompass a combination of persistent anxious thoughts, physical manifestations, and behavioral changes such as avoidance of once-routine activities. In particular, caffeine, substance abuse, and certain medications can exacerbate these symptoms (MedlinePlus, 2023). Diagnosis involves a thorough evaluation of symptoms, medical history, and physical examinations. Psychological evaluations performed by healthcare providers or mental health professionals further help understand and diagnose anxiety disorders.

Understanding Anxiety aims to demystify the intricate landscape of anxiety, offering insights into its various forms and practical strategies for coping with its challenges.

As we unravel the mysteries of anxiety, I invite you to join this exploration with your open heart and receptive mind. This book is more than just an examination of the various anxiety disorders; it seeks to become a guide that offers practical strategies that can be perfectly incorporated into everyday life. The pages that follow provide not only information about the nature of anxiety but also tangible tools that empower people to cope with and manage its impact.

The goals are ambitious but deeply rooted in the realm of the achievable: to provide a brief but comprehensive overview of anxiety disorders, to offer practical advice for coping with life with anxiety, and perhaps most importantly, to equip you with the tools necessary to improve your abilities. This book is an invitation to embrace change, an opportunity to open yourself to a new perspective, and a call to action to begin a journey toward understanding, empathy, and personal growth.

So, we will embark on this exploration together, transcending the limits that anxiety can impose, and discover the transformative power of understanding and managing anxiety for a more connected and fulfilled life.

Chapter 1:

A Journey of Exploration About

Anxiety

Welcome to the first stop on our journey: a deep dive into the basics of anxiety. Really understanding where these feelings come from is a fundamental part of learning the art of living with anxiety. Because even if we get this out of the room quickly, anxiety is hardly "eliminated." It is a reaction of our bodies and our minds to various situations in life, and it is necessary to conceive it as a natural part of being human. When you learn to live with it, but being the one in control of the vehicle, life becomes much easier.

Understanding the root of our anxiety also means that we must dive deep within ourselves. We are about to embark on an adventure of self-discovery, where we will unravel the threads of everything that happens to us. Thus, through self-knowledge, we will understand the nature of anxiety as we explore its various forms, and, most importantly, we will accept it as part of who we are.

You know, anxiety is like that quirky friend who shows up uninvited but always has something to say. Sometimes, what they say gives value to what we experience. As we will see throughout the book, anxiety can be a valuable ally when used well. But poorly provoked anxiety can be destructive. In this chapter, we will get to know this "friend" a little better, this passenger that we all carry inside. We will do this until we can recognize and accept it as a unique aspect of your being.

Brace yourself for a deep dive into the twists and turns of this complex emotion, unraveling the challenges that may have manifested in your life. As we navigate through the labyrinth of anxiety, we will confront the intricacies of your reactions and emotions, seeking to decipher the reasons behind them.

The path we are about to tread is uniquely yours, and together, we will navigate its contours. This isn't merely an exploration of anxiety in the abstract; it's a profound endeavor to harmonize with it as an integral part of your personal odyssey.

So, let's delve into the rich tapestry of your experiences, for understanding anxiety is more than just acknowledging it—it's about forging a connection with it as an inseparable element of your individual journey. We stand united on this expedition, committed to facing the challenges head-on and emerging stronger together.

Unmasking Anxiety: Understanding the Nature of Anxiety

Nature exhibits remarkable wisdom and complexity. Humans, despite our intelligence, struggle to comprehend much of it. We observe efficient designs in birds' flight, inspiring our aircraft. In our evolution, survival remains the fundamental goal.

The mystery of consciousness persists. It involves explaining the emergence of subjective sensations and awareness from physical and neural brain processes. Despite progress in neuroscience, this puzzle continues to baffle scientists and philosophers.

The complexity lies in the fact that, although we can understand how certain brain processes are associated with specific cognitive functions, such as memory or visual processing, it remains a mystery to explain why these processes are accompanied by subjective experiences. In other words, why should neural information processing give rise to the feeling of being conscious?

Scientists have, so far, taken different approaches to address this problem, from materialist perspectives that seek to explain consciousness in purely physical terms to more philosophical approaches that suggest that consciousness may have aspects that are irreducible and not fully explainable by current science.

The lack of consensus about the precise nature of consciousness and how it arises has led to a diversity of theories, from physicalism and functionalism to more radical ideas such as panpsychism, which proposes that consciousness is a fundamental property of the universe.

It is understood that anxiety arises as a response from our body to the need to survive, a kind of "human alarm system" that helps us respond to possible threats. This surprising and invasive feeling takes us out of lethargy and places us on the defensive. Our minds are naturally designed to respond to threats (Telch, n.d.).

As human beings, our existence is based mainly on everything we perceive around us. In the process of constructing your own conception of the universe, anxiety emerges as a complex and often elusive force. You can imagine it as that guest who appears without warning and makes their presence known in various ways. For those who commit to self-improvement and navigate the challenging terrain of anxiety, the journey will be recognized and appreciated.

Confronting an adversary as elusive as anxiety is certainly not an easy task. This intricate shadow lurks stealthily and is ready to launch its attack at the most inopportune moments. Sometimes, anxiety disguises itself as everyday stresses or in the aftermath of past traumas. You may find it lurking behind the veil of your daily worries. Its strategy is subtle, and its presence is often revealed late.

This adversary, although invisible to the naked eye, has a powerful impact on our psyche and emotional well-being. Facing this challenge requires courage and a deep understanding of the complexities of anxiety, an enemy that does not always present itself clearly and often eludes our attempts to fully understand it.

Understanding the nature of anxiety is a puzzle with pieces that often seem to shift, presenting a challenge that requires both intellect and emotional acuity. On this path, it is essential to recognize that understanding is not linear or uniform. Each individual's experience with anxiety is unique, and the solutions that result may vary. And always, absolutely in all cases, there is a learning curve.

In my case, I opted for humor, an underestimated ally, which became a welcome companion on this journey. With time and practice, you will learn to accept life's twists and turns with a touch of humor. After all, laughter is a universal language that transcends the barriers that anxiety tries to impose.

I also learned to understand the intricate dance between the causes and effects of anxiety. My diagnosis of anxiety disorders was late. Without even knowing it, I lived most of my life dealing with anxiety disorders. I mean, I knew something was up, but that "something" had no name, and therefore, I didn't know the tools to control (or counteract) these feelings. It's all about recognizing the triggers that set the stage for anxiety to set in and understanding the ripple effect it can have on our thoughts, emotions, and behaviors. At that moment, when we understand the root, we have the opportunity to cut off the anxious impulse.

Unmasking anxiety involves going deep and removing the fat from our minds. Ultimately, knowing our mind allows us to control anxiety. Disarm it of its power. Knowledge becomes ours as if up our sleeve, and understanding the dynamics of cause and effect is akin to mastering the art of strategic warfare against anxiety.

Remember that understanding is not a one-size-fits-all task. Seek professional guidance that aligns with your unique journey, and don't hesitate to add a dose of humor to the mix. Laughter, as they say, is the best medicine, and in the case of anxiety, it can be a powerful antidote.

Identifying Different Forms of Anxiety

Anxiety, that multifaceted emotional state that weaves its threads into the fabric of our lives, reveals itself in diverse ways, each with its own challenges and distinctive characteristics. This complex emotional framework has been the subject of study by researchers who, with their findings, have shed light on the intricate nature of this widespread phenomenon.

Each form of anxiety seems to be like a unique chapter in a book, each with its own plot and outcome. Some manifest themselves through excessive and persistent worry, while others manifest themselves through sudden and intense attacks.

They can affect deeply human aspects such as social interaction, leading to avoidance behaviors that can affect interpersonal relationships. They can also present as episodes of irrational fear, each with its own unique dynamics and triggers.

Next, we will see a more detailed approach to the different forms of anxiety in order to appreciate the richness and diversity of this emotional phenomenon. This means we will delve into the nuances of the human experience, recognizing that each form of anxiety has its own voice, its own story, and its own lesson.

Generalized Anxiety Disorder (GAD)

GAD, more than just an occasional concern, manifests itself as a constant and excessive worry about everyday aspects. The sphere of concern ranges from health to finances, work, and family dynamics.

Those who suffer from GAD often experience high levels of chronic anxiety, a constant presence that infiltrates their daily functioning. This disorder not only involves worry itself but also the weight that this emotional burden carries, significantly impacting quality of life and general well-being.

It can have various causes that include genetic factors, evidencing a possible hereditary predisposition towards the development of anxiety disorders. In addition, traumatic experiences, chronic stress, or challenging situations in the environment can significantly contribute to the emergence of these sensations.

Furthermore, imbalances in brain neurotransmitters, such as serotonin and norepinephrine, are also postulated as factors that play an important role in the appearance and persistence of this disorder. These elements interact in complex ways, underscoring the need for a holistic understanding to effectively address GAD.

Panic Disorder

Panic disorder, like a sudden emotional storm, is characterized by recurrent, unexpected attacks. These episodes, charged with intense and visceral fear, erupt without warning, creating an overwhelming feeling of imminent danger.

Panic attacks can be triggered by a variety of factors, including physiological changes such as hormonal fluctuations during the menstrual cycle or menopause, as well as medical problems such as hypoglycemia. Consuming substances such as caffeine, stimulants, alcohol, or illicit drugs can also increase the risk of experiencing panic attacks.

Triggering situations, such as claustrophobia or fear of flying, can evoke intense responses in susceptible people. It is crucial to recognize the variability in the interaction of these factors between individuals.

Understanding the underlying causes is critical to identifying and effectively treating panic attacks, often through approaches such as cognitive behavioral therapy, drug therapy, or a combination of both.

Panic attacks are not just limited to the moment they occur; their consequences can resonate in the long term, affecting confidence, personal security, and willingness to face everyday situations. The uncertainty associated with the sudden onset of these attacks adds an additional layer of complexity to the experience of panic disorder.

Social Anxiety Disorder (SAD)

In the theater of social anxiety, SAD unfolds its stage with an intense fear of social situations. This fear often translates into avoidance behaviors, limiting social interactions and affecting interpersonal relationships.

Previous experiences of rejection, teasing, or uncomfortable social situations can increase vulnerability to social anxiety disorder. In addition, a learning environment where fear of negative evaluation or overprotection has been instilled can also influence its development.

Personally, for a long time, when entering a room full of people, I had the mistaken belief that everyone was watching me, which aroused intense anxiety. This false perception fueled my social fears, but with time and proper treatment, I was able to learn to manage my anxiety, challenging those beliefs and significantly improving my quality of social and emotional life.

Social anxiety does not simply stop at occasional discomfort; rather, it can have a widespread impact on quality of life, restricting opportunities for personal and professional growth. Fighting the constant fear of judgment from others becomes a daily battle for those facing the challenge of SAD.

Specific Phobias

Specific phobias, although they may seem irrational to some, represent intense and debilitating fears of particular objects or situations. From the fear of heights to the aversion to certain animals or the fear of flying, these phobias have distinctive characteristics.

Experiencing a triggering situation for a person with phobias can be extremely dramatic, plunging them into an overwhelming emotional spiral. When the person is faced with fear, each detail or associated clue triggers a panic response. The mind is filled with frightening and often irrational thoughts, exacerbating anxiety and generating deep emotional discomfort.

This state of constant alertness to fear can affect the quality of life and limit daily activities. Compassionate understanding, seeking professional help, and applying adaptive coping strategies are critical in providing support to those facing the challenge of overcoming their phobias.

Exposure therapy, which gradually confronts and desensitizes the person to the feared object or situation, becomes a valuable tool in the treatment of these phobias. More than simple fears, specific phobias can significantly alter daily life and the decisions made to avoid these feared experiences.

Obsessive-Compulsive Disorder (OCD)

In the realm of OCD, intrusive thoughts and compulsions dance in a complex mental choreography. This disorder not only involves persistent worry (obsessions) but also the repetitive performance of mental acts or behaviors (compulsions).

When I started studying psychology and anxiety disorders, I recognized many of these behaviors in my life. Recognizing these obsessive behaviors was the first step toward understanding and accepting my own mind. Although I never experienced a full OCD diagnosis, this revelation motivated me to explore self-help strategies to address these patterns of thinking and behavior constructively.

Through this process, I learned to manage these behaviors in a healthier way, recognizing that we all have our idiosyncrasies and that self-discovery is an ongoing journey toward personal growth. Acceptance and understanding of these obsessive tendencies allowed me to cultivate greater compassion for myself and for those facing similar challenges on their journey toward mental balance.

The prevalence of OCD and its variability in symptom expression demand a personalized treatment approach. The constant fight against intrusive mental patterns and compulsive rituals turns OCD into an emotional battle, where proper understanding and support play an essential role in the path to recovery.

Post-Traumatic Stress Disorder (PTSD)

PTSD, as an indelible imprint of traumatic experiences, triggers intrusive memories, avoidance, and changes in cognition and emotional arousal. This disorder is not limited to the experience of the traumatic event itself; Its effects reverberate in daily life, affecting relationships, perception of the environment, and the ability to cope with stress.

It is true that many soldiers experience PTSD upon returning from the battlefield. The transition from a combat environment to civilian life can present significant challenges for these individuals, and they sometimes encounter limitations in reintegrating and interacting normally in society.

Difficulty re-engaging may be linked to several factors, such as overactivity of the stress response system, society's lack of understanding of the effects of war trauma, and feelings of isolation or disconnection. Stigmatization and lack of adequate support can also contribute to these limitations.

Successful reintegration of veterans may require a comprehensive approach that includes psychological support, counseling, and programs that facilitate adjustment to civilian life. Public awareness of the challenges faced by veterans with PTSD is essential to fostering the understanding and support needed in their reintegration process, allowing them to regain a fuller and more satisfying life in society.

The heterogeneity of PTSD symptoms underscores the need for a comprehensive understanding and targeted interventions that address the individual complexities of those struggling with the emotional aftermath of traumatic experiences.

Post-traumatic stress disorder isn't confined to military veterans; it can emerge from various traumatic experiences.

In my case, the source of my PTSD was an extended period of chronic stress in my workplace, characterized by the relentless mental abuse inflicted by a narcissistic alcoholic supervisor. Each day unfolded as a relentless struggle, pushing my nervous system into a perpetual fight-or-flight mode. The workplace environment became a relentless trigger, demanding constant reactions to navigate through the challenges.

When the problematic supervisor was eventually replaced, the change in environment did not bring immediate relief. It took some time after acquiring a new supervisor for the impact of the past experiences to manifest as PTSD and be formally diagnosed.

This experience underscores that a simple shift in surroundings doesn't automatically cure PTSD; the residual effects can persist, demanding a comprehensive approach to healing and recovery.

Embracing Change

Let's begin to consider the idea of embracing change as an invitation to rethink our relationship with anxiety and develop an adaptive and positive mindset to face our challenges.

To manage anxiety, you will see that the need for change becomes a call to action. It involves adopting an adaptive mindset and recognizing that while anxiety may be a natural response to stressful situations, it is also a dynamic force that we can influence. By embracing change, we are taking the first step toward a new way of approaching anxiety: not as an invincible enemy but as a moldable force that can be redirected toward more positive perspectives.

It is undeniable that anxiety is an inherent part of the human experience. Since our earliest days, anxiety has been our warning mechanism, our alarm signal in the face of imminent danger. However, this warning system, although vital, becomes a double-edged sword throughout life. Sometimes, anxiety drives us to overcome obstacles and prepare for the unknown. Other times, it becomes a burden, generating unreasonable fears and limiting our potential.

Are your fears an engine that drives positive change in your life, or have they become chains that limit you? Do you recognize the source and nature of your anxieties? Are they proportionate responses to situations, or are they sometimes unleashed disproportionately?

On this introspective journey, consider how your relationship with anxiety has evolved over the years. Has it been your ally in critical moments, or has it been a shadow that darkens your daily experiences? Recognizing the duality of anxiety is the first step to embracing change and beginning to build a more positive mindset.

It's time to see the glass as half full. Instead of seeing anxiety as a constant enemy, see it as an opportunity to grow and learn. I suggest you think about the worst possible scenario: Is it really as catastrophic as it seems? This perspective exercise can help you demystify your fears and find resilience in the face of adversity. Embrace the opportunity to transform anxiety from a paralyzing force into a catalyst for personal growth.

The Power of Acceptance

In the quest to control anxiety and conquer the shadows of past traumas, we often find ourselves entangled in a relentless struggle. The relentless search for control, an attempt to corral our fears and uncertainties, can ironically become a breeding ground for more distress. However, in the midst of the chaos, there is a profound lesson waiting to be learned: the profound strength that lies in the art of acceptance.

Acceptance is not an admission of defeat; rather, it is a brave recognition of reality. It is an invitation to face our anxieties with open arms, embracing them not as adversaries but as aspects of our human experience.

Understandably, this may seem like a daunting task because anxiety has a way of convincing us that we must constantly fight it. However, what if we changed our perspective and considered the possibility that acceptance could be our most powerful weapon? What happens when we remove "entity" from those feelings that overwhelm us? Well, they lose strength. They lose weight.

Acceptance can be a strong current that takes away what harms us. It does not require you to change the course of the river; instead, it encourages you to navigate the twists and turns with newfound grace and transformative force. Acceptance then means releasing the need for absolute control and recognizing that vulnerabilities and imperfections are not signs of weakness but rather the very fabric of our shared humanity.

One thing is certain, and we cannot escape it, and that is that the path to healing can be particularly challenging. Scars from the past can linger, haunting the present with echoes of pain. These traumas limit our lives even in the most basic aspects of daily life. Acceptance does not ask you to erase these scars but invites you to trace their contours with empathy and understanding. It is a strategy that assures you that your value goes far beyond the wounds you carry.

Another aspect where the power of acceptance lies is in giving up the illusion of control. It invites you to let go of the relentless pursuit of perfection and instead embrace the beautifully imperfect nature of life. This is not an endorsement of resignation but a declaration of strength: the strength to resist, evolve, and emerge resilient. A kind of "stoic vision" of our own existence, where what we do not control should not infer in any way in our lives.

Take a moment to breathe. Inhale the essence of acceptance, exhale the burdens of control. You are not alone in this search. Let acceptance be your compass, guiding you toward the serenity that comes from embracing every facet of your being, anxiety and all.

Building a Positive Mindset

Developing a positive mindset is crucial when it comes to dealing with anxiety. With the right mindset, people can learn to handle it and overcome it. How do we achieve that mentality? With practice, work, and commitment to the chosen path. It is a conscious decision, daily, to face challenges positively and trusting in ourselves. Below are some strategies to help develop a positive mindset when dealing with anxiety.

Self-awareness: As we learned earlier, you need to understand the triggers and patterns of your anxiety. By becoming aware of the specific causes of your anxiety, you can work to address those issues directly. For this, self-awareness is the necessary tool.

Practice the exercise of taking a second to "think about your thoughts" daily. Analyze what you feel. Become aware of your own being.

Positive affirmations: Incorporate positive affirmations into your daily routine. Repeat phrases that focus on your strengths, resilience, and ability to overcome challenges. Affirmations can help rewire your thinking patterns and prove effective in questioning and countering negative thoughts.

Repeating affirmations works for many people. It allows them to strengthen their minds and hearts and gives them courage to move forward. Remember that each strategy may work for some and not for others.

Practice gratitude: Cultivate the habit of gratitude. Periodically reflect and appreciate the positive aspects of your life. Gratitude is also a valuable tool for social interaction. Focusing on and being grateful for the positive aspects of your life can divert your attention from anxiety-provoking thoughts and create a more optimistic outlook.

Think of something positive in your life, and hold on to that. Incorporating this strategy into your life is about mastering the art of seeing the glass half full. Many people find writing in a gratitude journal to be helpful.

Mindfulness and meditation: Practice mindfulness and meditation to be present in the moment. Mindfulness techniques can help you disconnect from anxious thoughts and create a sense of calm.

Meditation, even just a few minutes a day, can contribute to a more focused and positive mindset. We will see some of its benefits later.

Challenge negative thoughts: This is also a little bit of what gratitude is about. The idea is that you actively challenge and reframe negative thoughts. And when I say actively, I mean that they are decisions that you make every day. When anxiety appears, question the validity of those thoughts and change them to more realistic and positive ones.

This cognitive restructuring can be a powerful tool for managing anxiety. As mentioned before, it is about learning to remove "weight" or "entity" from those thoughts that generate anxiety. Identifying a calm space and moment allows you to slow down and clear your mind, enabling focused reflection on your thoughts without disturbances.

Healthy lifestyle choices: Make sure you take care of your physical well-being. Regular exercise, a balanced diet, and enough sleep can have a positive impact on your mental health and contribute to a more resilient mindset.

For many people, food is a source of constant anxiety. Sometimes, eating seems to be the solution to satisfy those feelings, but at the end of the day, it turns out to be worse than the illness. That is why it is essential to have a positive view of yourself to avoid these types of falls.

Set realistic goals: Break tasks into smaller, achievable objectives to not feel overwhelmed. Celebrate your achievements, no matter how small, and use them as proof of your ability to overcome challenges.

If you set unattainable goals, you only generate frustration and anxiety. Therefore, it is a good strategy to really analyze what you want to achieve. Think in depth about how and when you will achieve it, and then decide.

Seek support: Don't hesitate to ask for help from friends, family, or a mental health professional. Talking about your feelings and experiences can give you a different perspective and help ease the burden of anxiety.

Professional therapy can assist you in learning how to introspect and comprehend factors that impact you in a negative way. You'll be able to quickly recognize the origin and act on the root of the matter.

Learn from setbacks: View setbacks as opportunities for growth. Instead of dwelling on perceived failures, view them as learning experiences that can contribute to your personal development.

Avoid dwelling on the past or worrying excessively about the future. Focus on the present moment and the positive actions you can take right now.

In the first chapter, we have explored the complex nature of anxiety, recognizing that it is a challenging experience that can affect different people in various ways. We also highlighted the importance of adopting a positive mindset as a foundation for coping with anxiety.

We discussed key strategies, such as self-awareness, to understand anxiety triggers and patterns, using positive affirmations to change thought patterns, and practicing gratitude and mindfulness to stay focused on the present.

We have also emphasized that overcoming anxiety involves an ongoing process and requires a constant commitment to practices that strengthen emotional resilience. Now, we will turn our attention to a specific aspect of anxiety: social anxiety.

In the next chapter, titled "Social Anxiety: The Art of Overcoming Obstacles," we will further explore social anxiety, a significant challenge for many.

We'll dive into specific tactics designed to overcome obstacles associated with anxiety in social situations. We'll cover how cultivating a positive mindset can play a crucial role in developing interpersonal trust and building healthy relationships.

Chapter 2:

Social Anxiety: The Art of

Overcoming Obstacles

In this chapter, which is dedicated to unraveling the social aspects of anxiety, the narrative delves into the intricate landscape of symptoms that characterize this complex condition.

At its core, social anxiety manifests as an overwhelming fear of social interactions, transforming everyday commitments into overwhelming challenges. The symptoms, both psychological and physical, are explored in detail, painting a vivid picture of the internal turmoil experienced by people struggling with this condition. In this art of triumphing over obstacles, individuals delve deeper into their own psyche, unraveling the intricate web of thoughts and emotions that fuel their fears.

Psychologically, social anxiety often manifests as persistent negative thoughts, intense shyness, and an incessant fear of judgment or scrutiny from others. These cognitive patterns contribute to a heightened sense of vulnerability in social situations, creating a pervasive and often paralyzing fear that inhibits one's ability to authentically relate to others.

Physically, the symptoms are equally striking and encompass a variety of manifestations, such as tremors, sweating, tachycardia (heart rate over 100 beats per minute), and even nausea. These responses serve as tangible indicators of the internal struggle faced by those with social anxiety, further intensifying the challenges that social interactions present.

Cognitive restructuring is a fundamental element that involves challenging and reframing negative thoughts. Identifying and challenging irrational beliefs paves the way for more balanced perspectives with the help of visualization techniques that mentally rehearse successful social interactions.

Complemented by relaxation techniques such as deep breathing and meditation, these practices control the physical manifestations of anxiety. It is about equipping ourselves with effective social skills as another key facet. Throughout this process, each step forward to confront and overcome social fears is recognized and commemorated.

It is necessary to understand that overcoming social anxiety is a gradual process as people find the confidence to navigate social interactions with increasing ease. The art of overcoming the obstacles associated with social anxiety is a personal and ongoing masterpiece that requires dedication, patience, and commitment to self-improvement.

As the narrative unfolds, it delves into the deep sense of isolation experienced by people struggling with social anxiety. Social interactions, normally seen as opportunities for connection and camaraderie, become fraught with apprehension and a sense of impending doom. The chapter explores the paradoxical nature of social anxiety, in which the innate human desire for connection collides with the paralyzing fear that social interactions can induce.

Isolation becomes a prevalent theme, as people with social anxiety often withdraw from social situations to avoid the discomfort and distress associated with them. The narrative illustrates how this isolation, although initially a coping mechanism, further exacerbates the sense of alienation and contributes to a cycle of avoidance.

Through relatable anecdotes and scenarios, this chapter illuminates the profound impact of social anxiety on an individual's perception of themselves and others. We paint a moving picture of the internal struggles faced by those navigating a world where the very essence of human connection becomes a source of deep anxiety. The chapter sets the stage for further exploration of strategies and techniques that form the art of overcoming these social obstacles, providing a ray of hope for those seeking to free themselves from the isolating clutches of social anxiety.

Decoding Social Anxiety

Social anxiety is a nuanced psychological phenomenon, and recognizing its symptoms is a crucial first step in understanding and addressing the condition. It is characterized by an intense fear of social interactions arising from a deep concern about the judgment and negative evaluation of others.

This constant worry about what others think creates a mental scenario in which every social interaction becomes an emotional challenge, a kind of scenario in which the perception of others is magnified.

You are in a constant state of alert, and your mind becomes an internal battlefield where social expectations and fear of other people's judgment intertwine. Every word spoken, every gesture, and every choice is subjected to rigorous personal scrutiny, fueling constant self-criticism. And above all, unnecessary mental exhaustion.

The weight of this worry becomes a challenge not only to interact with others but also to be true to oneself. Authenticity, which should be a fundamental pillar in human relationships, is threatened by the fear of disapproval. Social anxiety, in this context, becomes a constant companion, and the symptoms can manifest themselves both psychologically and physically.

Psychological Symptoms

1. *Persistent negative thoughts*

   Individuals grappling with social anxiety often find themselves caught in a web of persistent negative thoughts. These self-defeating cognitions create an internal dialogue that consistently anticipates the worst outcomes in social scenarios. The mind becomes a battleground of self-doubt and apprehension, amplifying the overall anxiety associated with social interactions.

2. *Intense self-awareness*

Social anxiety heightens self-awareness to an intense degree. The affected individuals become hyper-focused on their own behavior, actions, and perceived flaws. This heightened self-consciousness can lead to a pervasive sense of being under constant scrutiny, making even routine social encounters feel like daunting performances.

3. *Fear of judgment*

A fundamental characteristic of social anxiety is the deep-seated fear of judgment. Individuals afflicted by social anxiety harbor an overwhelming concern about being negatively evaluated or rejected by others. This fear can be paralyzing, influencing their decisions and behavior in an attempt to avoid potential criticism.

Physical Symptoms

1. *Trembling and shaking*

The physiological responses associated with social anxiety often manifest in noticeable trembling or shaking. These physical reactions are outward expressions of the heightened stress response triggered by anxiety-inducing social situations. The involuntary shaking becomes a visible manifestation of the internal turmoil experienced by individuals grappling with social anxiety.

2. *Sweating*

Excessive sweating, particularly in social contexts, serves as a tangible indicator of anxiety-induced arousal. The body responds to the heightened stress levels by increasing perspiration, contributing to discomfort and further intensifying the individual's self-consciousness in social settings.

3. *Rapid heartbeat*

Social anxiety triggers the body's fight-or-flight mechanism, leading to a rapid heartbeat. The physiological response of an accelerated heart rate is a direct result of the body's preparation for a perceived threat. This heightened cardiovascular activity is both a consequence of and a contributor to the overall physical discomfort experienced by those navigating social anxiety.

Emotional, Cognitive and Behavioral Aspects

Social anxiety significantly impacts emotional well-being, giving rise to a complex range of emotions that contribute to the complexity of this condition. The predominant emotion is fear, accompanied by increasing anxiety, especially when anticipating social events. Additionally, people may experience frustration and disappointment with themselves for not meeting perceived social expectations, further exacerbating their anxiety.

Cognitively, thought processes play a key role in shaping an individual's perception of themselves and their social interactions. Cognitive distortions, such as overgeneralization and catastrophizing, contribute to distorted perceptions of social situations. Selective attention focuses on perceived negative aspects and filters out positive or neutral signals.

At a behavioral level, social anxiety influences behavior, leading to the adoption of specific coping mechanisms and avoidance strategies. Avoidant behaviors, such as avoiding challenging situations, reinforce a cycle that exacerbates anxiety. Additionally, people may resort to safety behaviors, such as over-rehearsing or relying on specific rituals, as a means of managing anxiety in social contexts.

It is essential to comprehensively understand the emotional, cognitive, and behavioral aspects of social anxiety to decode the complexities of this condition. Recognizing the interaction between these components provides a crucial foundation for developing effective strategies to address and overcome social anxiety.

Facing Fear Head-On

When I think about the transformative power you will experience by facing your own fears head-on, I also think of the infinite sea of opportunities that will open up thanks to this change of mindset. Because it's the only way possible to do it. You will discover that fear acts as an indicator of the significance and challenge of your endeavors. Isn't that exactly what it's about? If you don't experience fear, wouldn't you be limiting your ability to take truly meaningful and transformative actions?

Fear, far from being an insurmountable obstacle, is your natural reaction. It is an intrinsic part of your psychology and is the engine that drives your advancement. It is fear that pushes you to explore the unknown, overcome seemingly insurmountable obstacles, and reach new heights. Thus, facing fear becomes a manifestation of your will to transcend your limitations and evolve.

A while back, a promising job opportunity came knocking, tempting me with the possibility of a new career and a complete life change—packing up my family and moving to a different state. Excitement bubbled up initially, but then doubts crept in about leaving the familiar behind. Despite the uncertainty, I believed this move could bring positive changes to my career and family life. It took some courage, but we eventually decided to take the plunge into the unknown.

The whole moving process was like a rollercoaster—exciting yet anxiety-inducing. We had so many questions. How would we adjust to the new place? Would my new job be a good fit? Could my kid adapt to a different school? Navigating through these concerns, we opted for temporary housing until the school year ended, considering the impact on our son's education.

We bought a new home, and I started my new job, only to find out that the work environment wasn't as great as I'd hoped. Each day became a struggle, and I couldn't help but think about the challenges my family was facing. As if that wasn't enough, just when we were ready to sell our old house, the COVID-19 pandemic hit, putting a pause on home viewings. The uncertainty about when we could sell the house added another layer of stress.

In those tough times, I turned to techniques found in this book—reflecting, meditating, and using affirmations. It led me to realize that the work environment wasn't acceptable, and I made the difficult decision to resign without another job lined up. Financial worries kicked in, turning this experience into a lesson in resilience and open-mindedness.

From then on, I started making decisions that were right for me, not just what others expected. We eventually sold our house, completed the move, and I found a job that I genuinely enjoy, surrounded by wonderful people. Confronting our fears not only helped us overcome challenges but also break free from the limitations we had placed on ourselves due to fear.

Brave Mindset

Developing the right mindset to deal with anxiety involves cultivating the courage to confront your own inner ghosts. Anxiety, at its core, is often rooted in irrational fears and negative anticipations. By embracing the courage to face these shadows, you not only demystify your fears but also give yourself the opportunity to learn, grow, and discover an inner strength that you may not have known you had.

When facing anxiety, a fundamental part of the process is facing fear. Not only will it transform your relationship with anxiety, but it will also empower you to embrace your life more fully. It is through this courageous confrontation that you will discover the ability to forge your own path, overcoming self-imposed barriers and unlocking the potential that can only be unleashed when you are willing to look directly into the eyes of your deepest fears.

In this brave confrontation, you will discover that starting the path to overcoming social anxiety requires a gradual approach. This gradual process will allow you to challenge your limits little by little. Remember that every little progress counts.

Gradual Approach Therapy

This therapeutic technique recognizes the need for a step-by-step process to desensitize individuals to feared social situations and gradually build trust.

In this approach, people start with small, manageable steps that expose them to mildly anxiety-provoking situations. The emphasis is on creating a hierarchy of social challenges, ranging from least to most anxiety-provoking scenarios. For example, starting a conversation with a person you know or practicing self-expression in a low-pressure environment can be the first steps.

Gradual exposure allows people to acclimate to social interactions without overwhelming anxiety. Over time, as they become successful in facing and handling less intimidating situations, they can gradually progress to more challenging situations. This method aligns with the principles of behavioral therapy, fostering a sense of accomplishment and empowerment as individuals witness their growing ability to navigate social contexts.

Facing fear head-on through gradual approach therapy is a dynamic process that recognizes the unique pace at which individuals confront and overcome social anxiety. It encourages resilience, patience, and a positive mindset, which ultimately leads to greater self-confidence in social settings.

Adopting this approach requires commitment and support, often involving guidance from mental health professionals specializing in cognitive-behavioral approaches. The therapeutic journey focuses not only on addressing immediate fears but also on equipping people with lasting tools to manage social anxiety in the long term.

Gradual approach therapy is a testament to the transformative power of facing fear head-on, providing a roadmap for people to regain the ability to control their social lives and free themselves from the limitations of social anxiety.

Breaking Down Isolation Patterns

Embracing the journey of breaking patterns of isolation in the midst of social anxiety is an incredibly brave step, and I want you to recognize the strength within you as you walk this path. It is these first steps that truly transform your life in the long term. It may seem like a small decision today, but over time, these small modifications to your habits make immense progress.

As you take each step, start with small, manageable interactions, allowing yourself the grace to acclimate to the discomfort at your own pace. Social interactions often weave a complex web of fears: the fear of judgment, rejection, or the uncomfortable light of shame. Understanding these roots is like shedding light on the shadows, recognizing the emotions that contribute to your inclination to withdraw from social interactions.

Systematic desensitization, when faced with increasingly challenging social situations, becomes a gentle unfolding of your resilience and inner strength. This is how you begin to see the fruit of your work. This is how you begin to harvest your crops. This journey is yours, and it is essential to recognize that every small victory, every small step forward, is a triumph worth celebrating.

You are not alone in this, and the narrative you weave about yourself deserves to be one of kindness and understanding. Challenge negative self-talk with self-compassion. As you actively reframe these thoughts, visualize the emergence of a more positive and realistic personal narrative. Every attempt matters, no matter how small. The essential thing is that you find the courage to take the initiative and move towards others.

Social skills training is not just about learning techniques; It is a profound act of self-investment. Watch how, step by step, these skills strengthen you, reducing the need for isolation.

In this empathetic space, as you unfold the layers of isolation, I want you to know that every effort you make matters. You are not only breaking patterns of isolation; you are reclaiming the vibrant tapestry of human connection, one brave step at a time.

Overcoming Social Avoidance

Social avoidance refers to a pattern of behavior characterized by intentional withdrawal or avoidance of social interactions and situations. People who experience social avoidance often show a reluctance to engage with others due to feelings of discomfort, anxiety, or fear associated with social environments. Overcoming this obstacle requires a determined and gradual approach, focusing on building confidence and honing essential social skills.

The importance of social avoidance lies in its potential impact on personal well-being and the quality of relationships. Avoidance can contribute to feelings of isolation, hinder personal growth, and limit opportunities to form meaningful connections. Understanding and addressing social avoidance is crucial to fostering healthy social interactions, improving overall mental health, and promoting a more fulfilled life.

The first crucial step in this journey is understanding the roots of social avoidance, which involves delving into one's psyche and identifying negative thought patterns that contribute to anxiety. Reflecting on past experiences provides valuable information about fears and concerns that may prevent an individual from engaging in social interactions.

Second, you can start the process by going forward with small steps, gradually increasing the complexity of social situations so you can build trust. Attending low-key meetings or engaging in informal conversations with acquaintances provides a foundation on which to build more ambitious social goals.

We saw in the last chapter how challenging negative thoughts is a fundamental aspect of overcoming social avoidance, replacing self-defeating thoughts with positive, realistic affirmations, and accepting imperfections as part of the human experience.

As a fourth step, incorporating practices such as deep breathing and staying present in the current moment helps alleviate anxiety associated with past experiences or future uncertainties. Mindfulness fosters a sense of calm and facilitates a more focused approach to social situations.

Developing social skills is the fifth step in this transformative journey. Actively working on communication, honing active listening skills, and becoming an expert at interpreting non-verbal cues are crucial aspects of developing social competence. Joining social groups or participating in activities aligned with personal interests provides a natural environment to hone these skills.

Seeking support from trusted friends, family, or a therapist is the sixth step. Having a support network offers encouragement, guidance, and a sense of security during difficult times. Sharing goals and progress with others fosters a collaborative and nurturing environment that can significantly contribute to overcoming social avoidance.

Gradual exposure to different social situations is the seventh step. Desensitizing yourself to social anxiety involves starting with less intimidating scenarios and progressively increasing the complexity of interactions. This step helps develop resilience and adaptability, crucial attributes for navigating the complexities of social dynamics.

No matter how small, cheer for yourself. That is the eighth step. Recognizing progress increases self-esteem and maintains motivation throughout the journey. Regularly reflecting on achievements reinforces positive changes and provides a tangible record of progress made in overcoming social avoidance.

Learning from setbacks is the ninth step. Accepting setbacks as inherent to the learning process reframes them as opportunities for growth. Analyzing what went wrong, adjusting strategies if necessary, and applying lessons learned to future interactions contribute to a continuous cycle of improvement.

Finally, patience and perseverance serve as the cornerstone of this transformative journey. Overcoming social avoidance is a gradual process that requires commitment and resilience. The path to overcoming social avoidance is a multifaceted process that requires introspection. By following the steps outlined, people can free themselves from the constraints of social avoidance, expand their comfort zones, and build a more connected and enriched life.

In this chapter, we have explored the depths of social anxiety, unraveling the difficulties faced by those who suffer from it. From the constant stream of negative thoughts to the physical symptoms that accompany this condition, we have outlined a comprehensive overview of its challenges. However, by diving into this analysis, we have also highlighted the importance of addressing social anxiety gradually and facing fears progressively.

The key is to understand that overcoming social anxiety is not a one-way street but rather a journey of self-discovery and personal growth. Accepting initial discomfort and moving step by step toward challenging social situations is essential. The gradual exposure and progressive confrontation of fears allow for a more solid development and a more effective adaptation to the complexity of social interactions.

In the next chapter, we'll dive into an arsenal of tools and strategies designed to build your confidence. From stress management techniques to cognitive approaches, we'll explore various ways to build a strong foundation that empowers you against social anxiety. Get ready to discover how to transform challenges into opportunities and move towards a more confident and connected version of yourself in the exciting next chapter.

Chapter 3:

Tools to Strengthen Your

Confidence

Building confidence is not just about superficial self-assurance but goes deeper into the core of one's self-perception and belief system. It involves developing internal resilience that allows people to face life's uncertainties and challenges with a sense of capability and self-esteem. This process involves accepting one's strengths, recognizing achievements, and fostering a mindset that encourages growth and learning.

It is not easy, nor are there magic solutions. Achieving full strength of self-confidence is the result of a long and complex but achievable process. It means that you went through and overcame challenges one after the other, and that gives you confidence.

Confidence acts as a powerful antidote to the debilitating effects of anxiety, especially in challenging contexts. When people have a strong foundation of self-confidence, they are better equipped to confront and manage anxious thoughts and feelings. This feeling provides a buffer against the fear of being judged, allowing people to engage in social interactions more authentically and with a greater sense of ease.

We will see that, to appear safe in the face of anxiety, people expend valuable resources that could better be embarked on a journey of self-discovery, challenging and reframing negative thought patterns and gradually exposing themselves to feared situations. In this way, trust becomes a guiding force that allows them to navigate the complexities of social interactions with courage and resilience.

Throughout this chapter, we will see different strategies, approaches, and practical exercises that serve to strengthen self-confidence. This way, we can communicate more effectively with people who suffer from anxiety, and we ourselves will better understand the dynamics. Let's go for it!

Cultivating Inner Strength

Inner strength encompasses the inner strength and confidence inherent in every individual, including yourself. It involves skillfully managing your behavior by navigating thoughts and emotions in a healthy way, taking advantage of it to achieve goals and lead a rewarding life. When personal power remains untapped, decision-making and goal pursuit become challenging.

Overwhelmed by obstacles and setbacks, recovering from failures becomes a struggle. Problems such as low self-esteem, difficulty asserting yourself, and ineffective communication can arise. In addition, susceptibility to external influences and the inability to defend personal beliefs may prevail. The absence of personal power can lead to a feeling of stagnation both personally and professionally, making it difficult to realize your full potential.

Instead, embrace personal power to facilitate facing challenges with resilience and grace. It enhances effective communication, fosters strong relationships, and paves the way for success in various aspects of life. While some may categorize inner power as a "soft" skill, it is a cornerstone of success and leadership.

Essential to achieving aspirations, the power of self-confidence allows you to clearly visualize goals and execute actions to transform them into reality. You become more effective in every way. Doubt and fear can be overcome more quickly, allowing for sustained focus and motivation even in the face of adversity. The importance of strengthening self-confidence occupies a central place in this book, and we will see it throughout the following chapters.

We will discover that this path is not a mere exercise in vanity or superficial self-confidence. We are talking about a profound journey of self-discovery and empowerment, which involves the cultivation of a positive self-image, belief in one's own capabilities, and resilience in the face of challenges. Beyond a simple increase in self-esteem, this process takes time. We'll find together the development of unwavering confidence in one's ability to face the complexities of life with poise and conviction.

We must understand self-confidence as the cornerstone of personal growth and well-being. It is the force that drives people to take on new challenges, seize opportunities, and recover from setbacks. In the face of life's uncertainties, a strong sense of self-confidence acts as a guiding light and provides the courage to face fears, pursue ambitions, and thrive in the midst of adversity.

Self-Reflection for Confidence Building

The journey toward self-discovery and resilience is encapsulated in the art of cultivating self-reflection. It is a transformative process that transcends the superficial and delves into the deepest part of the being. This book explores the multifaceted aspects of cultivating self-reflection, from embracing self-compassion to celebrating personal growth, and highlights its profound impact on life's path.

The foundation of cultivating self-reflection is the acceptance of self-compassion. In a world that often demands perfection, being kind to yourself in times of challenge or failure becomes a powerful act of resilience. Recognizing imperfections as integral components of the human experience lays the foundation for a resilient mindset that can weather the storms of life.

A growth mindset is the cornerstone of cultivating self-reflection. Reframe challenges as opportunities for learning and growth, fostering adaptability and belief in the capacity for development. This mindset allows people to see setbacks not as obstacles but as stepping stones on the path to self-discovery and strength.

Positive affirmations emerge as powerful tools to reshape internal dialogue and reinforce a positive self-image. By consistently affirming their capabilities, value, and potential, individuals build a mental landscape that builds confidence and resilience. This practice acts as a continuous source of motivation to face life's countless challenges.

Mindfulness practices, such as meditation and deep breathing, infuse daily life with present-moment awareness. These practices cultivate self-reflection by reducing stress, improving emotional resilience, and providing a sanctuary for self-reflection. Mindfulness becomes a compass that guides people through the complexities of their inner landscapes.

Setting and pursuing authentic goals aligned with one's values becomes a testament to inner strength. The journey toward these goals is marked by determination, purpose, and an unwavering commitment to personal growth. Authenticity in goal setting fosters a sense of meaning and fulfillment, which helps strengthen the inner core.

Adversity, seen through the lens of self-reflection, is transformed into opportunity. The ability to face challenges with resilience and a forward-looking perspective becomes a hallmark of self-reflection. Adapting to adversity not only shapes character but also strengthens the internal resolve to face future uncertainties. Accepting vulnerability is an integral part of cultivating self-reflection. Authenticity and self-reflection are not mutually exclusive; Vulnerability is a conduit to deeper connections and a deeper understanding of oneself. It is a courageous recognition of oneself, fostering an authentic and resilient spirit.

The journey to cultivate self-reflection is a deep and ongoing process. It is not simply a personal effort; It becomes a ripple effect that positively influences the world around us and inspires others on their own journeys of self-discovery.

The Benefits of Self-Reflection

Often, limiting beliefs act as invisible barriers to self-confidence. Through introspection, one can identify and challenge these beliefs, replacing them with empowering narratives that contribute to a more positive self-perception.

It also provides a platform to examine the triggers of our anxiety, unraveling what lies beneath. As we have already seen in other chapters, a complete understanding of what happens to us is key to reach success.

Authentic self-confidence is closely tied to aligning one's actions with personal values. Through self-reflection, people can evaluate whether their behaviors and choices align with their core values. This alignment creates a congruence that enhances personal integrity, laying the foundation for a more authentic and confident self.

Self-reflection prompts an honest assessment of strengths and areas of growth. While recognizing and leveraging strengths contributes to confidence, recognizing areas of growth fosters a growth mindset. Adopting the path of continuous improvement improves self-confidence by emphasizing development potential.

If you incorporate these strategies into your daily routine, self-reflection becomes a guiding light on the path to building self-confidence. As a continuous and intentional practice, self-reflection becomes a transformative tool, laying the foundation for a safe and empowered journey of self-discovery.

The Balance Between Personal Effort and External Support

On the journey towards self-confidence, the tools presented in this book stand as solid foundations. However, it is imperative to understand the intricate dance between individual effort and external support. Taking on the challenge of self-discovery, actively applying these tools, and seeking encouragement from a support network form a robust foundation for improving self-confidence.

It means respecting the authenticity of the journey towards self-confidence since much of it lies in personal effort. Taking time to reflect, setting realistic goals, and committing to individual growth are crucial. Conscious self-exploration, supported by deliberate actions, becomes the cornerstone of overcoming social anxiety.

However, loneliness in this process is not an obligation. I would even say it's a disadvantage. Seeking support from friends, family, or even professionals can provide valuable perspectives. It is a support network that will give you support in the necessary moments, perhaps with a word, a hug, or simply being there with you. In this way, sharing experiences, receiving guidance, and feeling supported create an environment conducive to personal flourishing. Connecting with others can offer an external view, illuminating aspects that might escape individual perception.

Each step taken in the search for inner security is enriched by incorporating the wisdom and support of those around us. This harmonious balance paves the way that not only builds self-confidence but also weaves meaningful human connections into the fabric of life.

Strategies to Incorporate the Opinion of Others

Request constructive feedback: Acting boldly by asking for constructive feedback from those we trust can provide objective insight. Asking about our strengths and areas of improvement provides an opportunity for personal growth and continued adaptation.

Share goals and achievements: Opening up about personal goals and celebrating accomplishments with friends and loved ones strengthens bonds and fosters mutual support. Sharing the process of building trust allows you to receive encouragement and external perspectives that nourish your sense of personal achievement.

Participate in support groups: Joining specific support groups, whether in person or online, provides a safe space to share experiences. Interacting with people facing similar challenges provides a sense of belonging and offers practical strategies for overcoming social anxiety.

How to Deal With People With Anxiety?

Anxiety can become a lonely experience, leading the affected person to isolate themselves due to the emotional intensity they experience. Understanding anxiety can be difficult if you haven't experienced it, making it crucial to offer words of support. In this chapter, we will explain what to say to a person with anxiety, recognizing the complexity of their thoughts and emotions.

Firstly, to know what to say to a person with anxiety, it is essential to understand what anxiety entails and recognize its signs. This knowledge will allow you to identify when a friend, family member, partner or colleague is experiencing fear or concern. Furthermore, it is vital to differentiate between a panic attack, characterized by intense fear and temporary physical symptoms, and generalized anxiety, which persists over time with constant worries.

Sometimes the best intentions can backfire if the right words are not chosen. Although from an outside perspective they may seem harmless, people experiencing anxiety may interpret them differently. Anxiety and fear are genuine emotions, and what is said can significantly affect the affected person's perception.

Strategies for Treating Others' Anxiety

Provide constructive feedback: Offer feedback that is specific, constructive, and that emphasizes both strengths and areas for improvement. Foster a growth mindset by framing challenges as opportunities for learning and personal development rather than insurmountable obstacles.

Promote self-compassion: Create an environment that promotes self-compassion. Encourage people to treat themselves with kindness and understanding, challenging the harsh self-criticism that often accompanies low self-confidence.

Provide positive affirmations: Introduce positive affirmations that counter negative self-talk. Regularly repeating affirmations that highlight strengths and abilities helps people reconfigure their thinking patterns, reinforcing a more positive self-image.

Promote skills development: Promote the development of specific skills and competencies. Acquiring new skills not only improves confidence but also provides tangible evidence of one's abilities, contributing to a positive self-perception.

Be a supportive presence: Act as a consistent and supportive presence. Knowing that there is someone who believes in their abilities and is there to offer encouragement can significantly boost a person's confidence as they face challenges.

Tools to Strengthen Your Inner Confidence: Unleash Your Potential

Embarking on the journey to fortify your confidence might appear daunting, but rest assured, you're on the brink of reaching new heights! Here are some companionable tools to navigate this exhilarating path.

To kick things off, let's talk about positive affirmations—consider them as warm embraces for your mind, countering doubts, and skillfully weaving an optimistic and empowering narrative.

Now, cultivate a growth mindset, where each day becomes an adventure of self-discovery. Confront your fears gradually, allowing for the desensitization of responses and the gradual construction of confidence with every audacious stride. Remember, failure is not a dead-end; it's a launchpad for learning and growth.

Don't shy away from seeking constructive feedback; consider it a detailed map leading you to the treasure trove of personal development. Surround yourself with positive influences that genuinely believe in the vastness of your potential.

Harnessing the Power of Body Language

Effective communication extends beyond words; it involves the powerful realm of body language. When navigating social interactions, particularly for those grappling with anxiety, understanding and harnessing the influence of body language can be a transformative skill.

1. *Non-verbal confidence*

   Body language speaks volumes about confidence. Maintaining good posture, making eye contact, and having open gestures can convey self-assurance. For individuals dealing with anxiety, consciously adopting these confident postures not only influences how others perceive them but also triggers a positive feedback loop, fostering inner confidence over time.

2. *Activate listening cues*

   Engaging in meaningful conversations requires active listening. Non-verbal cues such as nodding, leaning slightly forward, and maintaining an open stance signal attentiveness. For those managing anxiety, focusing on these cues helps redirect attention from internal worries to the present interaction, facilitating a more genuine and less anxiety-inducing exchange.

3. *Managing nervous energy*

   Anxiety often manifests physically, leading to restless movements or fidgeting. Harnessing body language involves channeling nervous energy into purposeful actions. For instance, replacing fidgeting with intentional gestures or employing controlled movements can help individuals project a composed exterior, reducing the visible signs of anxiety.

4. *Mirroring and building connections*

   Mirroring, subtly mimicking the body language of the person you're interacting with, establishes a sense of rapport. It creates an unspoken connection and harmony in the interaction. For those contending with anxiety, mirroring can serve as a tool to ease social tension and enhance feelings of connection, as it aligns with the natural rhythms of social dynamics.

5. *Calming signals*

Understanding and utilizing calming body language signals can be invaluable in managing anxiety during social interactions. Slow, deliberate movements, controlled breathing, and maintaining a relaxed facial expression send signals not only to others but also to the mind, fostering a sense of calmness and control.

Facing Self-Doubt

This phenomenon, characterized by persistent self-doubt and fear of being exposed as a fraud despite evidence of success, is an obstacle that many people face in their personal and professional lives. Doubt has a way of permeating our thoughts and clouding our abilities. Among the various forms it takes, one particularly challenging manifestation is imposter syndrome. To confront self-doubt head-on, people must engage in a process of introspection to identify the roots of their insecurities. Uncovering the origins of these feelings can be a crucial step in understanding the irrationality of imposter syndrome and dismantling its hold.

Overcoming impostor syndrome involves a profound change in mentality. This transformation requires recognizing and internalizing one's own achievements, attributing success to personal capabilities and not to external factors. Adopt a growth mindset. That's what it's about. Living our lives immersed in a mindset in which challenges are considered opportunities for learning and development fosters resilience in the face of doubt.

Cultivating self-confidence is an ongoing journey and there are practical strategies to strengthen your sense of worth. Seeking mentoring and guidance from peers can provide external validation and perspective, helping to counteract the isolating nature of imposter syndrome. It is a journey toward recognizing one's own worth, accepting one's achievements, and reframing challenges as stepping stones rather than obstacles.

Overcoming Imposter Syndrome

Imposter syndrome, a psychological phenomenon first identified in 1978, has affected approximately 70% of people at some point in their lives, according to a study published in the International Journal of Behavioral Science (Sakulku & Alexander, 2011). Notable figures who have shared their experiences with this syndrome include actress Kate Winslet, singer Jennifer Lopez, lawyer and writer Michelle Obama, and astronaut Neil Armstrong.

This peculiar syndrome manifests itself significantly in high-performance individuals. Despite having tangible evidence of their abilities and achievements, these people experience persistent feelings of inadequacy and insecurity. The most striking thing is that, instead of attributing their successes to their own merit, they tend to attribute them to external factors such as luck or intense effort.

Professor Eva Rimbau, human resources expert and professor of Economics and Business Studies at the Universitat Oberta de Catalunya (UOC), highlights that this subjective perception is not supported by objective evidence or real indicators. Even though their career paths refute these feelings, those affected by imposter syndrome continue to attribute their achievements to external circumstances (Catalunya, n.d.).

The erroneous message that failure is not an option can prevail. The lack of open discussion about failures and obstacles on the path to success may contribute to this distorted perception. Professor Rimbau points out the importance of normalizing and recognizing setbacks and failures as a natural part of the process, questioning why there is not more open talk about how to overcome challenges and persevere in the pursuit of success.

The effects of impostor syndrome are far-reaching and infiltrate various aspects of an individual's life. Confidence, the cornerstone of personal and professional success, becomes a victim of the syndrome. The constant fear of being unmasked as unworthy undermines self-confidence, leading to a perpetual cycle of anxiety and decreased confidence. This doubt affects decision-making, hinders the pursuit of opportunities, and prevents people from fully realizing their potential. This phenomenon transcends age, gender, and profession, creating a pervasive sense of self-doubt that hinders personal and professional growth.

To challenge and overcome the feelings of inadequacy associated with imposter syndrome, people must first recognize and accept these emotions. Self-reflection becomes a powerful tool for unraveling the roots of these feelings, exposing the irrationality of the doubts that have taken root. Understanding that imposter syndrome is a common experience and not a personal flaw helps people normalize their struggles, fostering a sense of unity in the face of shared challenges.

Possible Strategies and Solutions to Impostor Syndrome

Changing your mindset is a crucial aspect of overcoming imposter syndrome. Affirmations and positive self-talk play a vital role in challenging negative thought patterns and encouraging more constructive self-talk. Adopting a growth mindset, in which challenges are seen as learning opportunities rather than accusations of inadequacy, contributes to the transformation of self-perception.

Practical strategies for building trust can be instrumental in overcoming imposter syndrome.

- Seeking mentorship and guidance from those who have faced similar challenges can provide valuable insight and external validation. Additionally, setting realistic goals and celebrating incremental successes contribute to a sense of accomplishment, gradually rebuilding the foundation of trust that imposter syndrome erodes.

- Case studies of people who have successfully overcome imposter syndrome serve as beacons of inspiration and practical guidance. It's about sharing stories of resilience. These individuals have not only confronted the impostor within but have emerged stronger, armed with new confidence and a deeper understanding of their capabilities.

- Recognize when you should feel like an imposter. Feeling part of a group contributes to confidence. If you're the only person in a meeting, classroom, field, or workplace who stands out, it's natural that from time to time, you'll feel like you don't quite fit in.

- Highlight the positive. Being a perfectionist indicates that you care deeply about the quality of your work. The key is to strive for excellence when it is crucial, but not obsess over routine tasks and forgive yourself when you make inevitable mistakes.

- Develop a healthy response to failure and making mistakes. Instead of beating yourself up for not measuring up, learn from the loss, just like players on a losing team do, and move on, reminding yourself, "Next time, I'll do better."

- Adjust the rules. If you've been following the wrong rules, like "I should always know the answer" or "never ask for help," it's time to assert your rights. Recognize that you have the same right as anyone else to make a mistake, have a bad day, or ask for assistance.

- Create a new script. Be aware of the self-talk when you face situations that trigger your imposter feelings. Break the cycle of constantly seeking external validation by learning to recognize your own achievements and congratulate yourself.

- Sometimes we all have to improvise. Instead of seeing "winging it" as showing your ineptitude, learn to see it as a skill, as many achievers do. Courage comes from taking risks. Change your behavior first and allow your confidence to build.

In conclusion, exploring various tools for strengthening self-confidence is critical to dealing effectively with anxiety.

Throughout this chapter, we have examined strategies ranging from positive affirmation to setting achievable goals, highlighting the importance of cultivating strong self-esteem as a foundation for addressing emotional challenges.

Strengthening our confidence is entirely up to us. In this way, we not only develop greater resilience in the face of anxiety but also improve our ability to face difficult situations with a positive and empowering mindset.

In the next chapter, we will explore how anxiety can affect our interpersonal relationships and provide effective strategies for navigating this challenge. We will discuss the importance of making meaningful connections while coping with anxiety and address how self-confidence can play a crucial role in building and maintaining healthy relationships.

We will aim to understand how anxiety can influence our social interactions. The idea is to finish this next chapter better equipped to cultivate meaningful connections and foster positive relationships on our journey to emotional well-being.

Chapter 4:

Navigating Anxiety for Meaningful Relationships

The importance of having meaningful emotional relationships in life cannot be underestimated. These connections not only provide emotional support but also add a deep sense of belonging and meaning. Close and meaningful relationships act as fundamental pillars that support our emotional health and contribute to our overall well-being. They are a big part of what it means to be human.

When we immerse ourselves in meaningful relationships, we find a space where we can express our authenticity, be understood, and be supported in our joys and challenges. These connections offer us an emotional safety net that helps us deal with difficult times and celebrate achievements. Additionally, they provide a sense of purpose and contribute to building a life support network.

However, it is important to recognize how anxiety disorders can make it difficult to bond with the people who matter most to us. Anxiety, with its varied manifestations, can create barriers to communication, create misunderstandings, and make it difficult to share our deepest thoughts and feelings. Constant worry and anticipation of stressful situations can lead to emotional disconnection, negatively affecting the quality of our relationships.

It is crucial to address the challenges that anxiety presents in the area of emotional relationships. Those facing anxiety disorders can benefit greatly from seeking support from loved ones and sharing their experiences. In turn, loved ones can play a key role by educating themselves about anxiety, fostering empathy, and offering a supportive environment.

This chapter delves into the intricate intersection of anxiety and our most intimate and meaningful relationships. For starters, the need to recognize that anxiety can profoundly affect the way we connect with others. The chapter aims to shed light on how anxiety can manifest in the context of close relationships, providing readers with ideas and strategies to foster healthy connections.

Because anxiety has the potential to influence our perceptions, communication styles, and overall emotional well-being, it is essential to address these dynamics within the realm of personal relationships. We will look at the delicate balance between vulnerability and self-preservation, emphasizing the importance of open communication and empathy to create a supportive environment.

Building on the foundation laid in previous discussions of strengthening self-esteem, the narrative highlights how a resilient sense of self can contribute to more secure and satisfying connections with others. We will do a comprehensive exploration of practical tools and insights for managing anxiety in the context of relationships.

From effective communication strategies to coping mechanisms that promote understanding and patience, the chapter seeks to equip people with the skills necessary to navigate the complexities of anxiety while fostering and maintaining meaningful relationships.

Building Genuine Connections

As individuals, the longing for genuine connections becomes even more vital for those who suffer from anxiety. Anxiety, with its complex manifestations, can color social interactions with shades of fear and constant worry. In this context, authenticity stands as a beacon of security in the midst of the emotional storms that often accompany anxiety disorders.

We know that human relationships can be a complex labyrinth of comings and goings. Although many times, it depends on one's own projection towards others. At the base of these relationships lies the building of genuine connections. These connections go beyond simple friendships and delve into the realms of authenticity and healthy dynamics. When we talk about "genuine," I mean that they are bonds in which you are just as you feel. They are those types of relationships where you can show yourself naturally, and you don't have to be planning every movement or word.

People who struggle with anxiety find authentic connections a refuge where they can let go of the masks and be accepted for who they truly are. Authenticity becomes an escape, allowing worries and fears to be shared openly, stripped of the weight of judgment. By opening up authentically, those facing anxiety can experience emotional relief as they feel fully understood and accepted.

The importance of recognizing healthy relationships becomes even more relevant in this context. Connections that promote an environment of understanding and support are essential to counteract the challenges that anxiety can pose in social interactions. Here, recognition of limits and patience take on a crucial role, providing a space where the person with anxiety can feel supported without feeling overwhelmed.

In the process of building genuine connections, empathy becomes an invaluable tool. Those who interact with people who suffer from anxiety can play a significant role in educating themselves about the nature of these disorders and fostering a supportive environment. Patience and a willingness to adapt to changing needs are essential elements in fostering healthy relationships that thrive on authenticity.

Ultimately, for those dealing with anxiety, healthy, authentic connections can be beacons of stability and emotional support. Building relationships based on authenticity and understanding provides a critical safety net, helping to dispel the shadows of anxiety and allowing the light of meaningful connections to illuminate the path to emotional well-being.

The Importance of Authenticity

Authenticity is, without a doubt, the cornerstone of any meaningful connection. When people allow themselves to be authentic in their relationships, it builds a solid foundation of trust and mutual understanding. This brave act involves accepting the vulnerability inherent in the human condition, sharing both our strengths and weaknesses, and allowing others to see us in our entirety.

In a world that sometimes favors superficial appearances, authentic connections stand out as beacons of sincerity, creating a safe space where people can freely express their thoughts, emotions, and aspirations without fear of judgment.

These authentic connections are not only liberating but also sustainable. By engaging authentically, we foster reciprocity, cultivating an environment where all participants feel valued and accepted. Within these genuine connections, personal growth is fueled as people are encouraged to explore and express their true potential.

It is about building authentic connections thanks to courage and effort, betting that the emotional and supportive benefits that emerge are invaluable. Facing anxiety openly and authentically can not only strengthen relationships but also demystify the perception that vulnerability is a weakness, transforming it into a powerful force for human connection.

Recognizing Healthy Relationships

Recognizing when a connection becomes toxic is a challenge we often face with reluctance and resistance. Each individual is a unique universe, with diverse experiences, emotions, and strengths that influence the way they perceive and manage their relationships. Not everyone has the same emotional strength to recognize and take action against the toxicity that can infiltrate their closest relationships.

Often, the difficulty in identifying a toxic relationship lies in the emotional proximity we establish with the other person. Emotions, shared history, and hope for change can cloud our judgment, preventing us from clearly seeing destructive patterns. On other occasions, they have to do with our own or inherited self-destructive patterns. The strength necessary to face healthy relationships means traveling a path full of obstacles, where acceptance of reality can be painful and, in many cases, overwhelming.

However, it is essential to remember that each step towards freedom from a toxic relationship is an act of courage. Not everyone has the ability to remove themselves from harmful situations immediately. Some need time to process and understand the toxicity that surrounds them, and it is vital to respect that individual process. True transformation occurs when, after freeing yourself from the bonds of a toxic relationship, you experience the fullness of a healthy connection.

It is at this moment that perception becomes clear, and the difference between the destructive and the constructive becomes evident. The feeling of well-being, mutual support, and joint growth becomes the compass that guides toward healthier relationships.

Once you have experienced the joy of a positive relationship, there is no turning back. Healthy parameters are established that serve as references, building a firm ground where toxicity has no place. Recognizing and embracing a healthy relationship not only means moving away from what is harmful but also learning to value and cultivate connections that contribute to emotional well-being and personal growth.

The journey to healthier relationships begins with self-awareness and a willingness to face reality, even when it is uncomfortable. Every individual deserves to experience connections that nourish their well-being, and by recognizing the importance of healthy relationships, the door opens to a fuller and more satisfying life.

Building genuine connections is a task that requires sensitivity to discern and nurture healthy relationships. In these relationships, mutual respect, effective communication, and a shared commitment to growth and well-being are essential. Recognizing a healthy relationship involves being attentive to the balance between giving and receiving, understanding limits, and valuing the uniqueness of each individual in that connection.

In healthy relationships, there is always room for open dialogue, constructive feedback, and celebration of individual successes. These connections act as refuges of support in difficult times and scenes of shared happiness during triumphs.

Fostering healthy relationships means continually committing to open communication, personal reflection, and dedication to promoting the well-being of everyone involved. Each step in this journey is an opportunity to create deeper and more meaningful bonds, enriching the lives of all participants in the process.

Anxiety in Romantic Relationships

Anxiety in romantic relationships can manifest itself in a variety of ways, from the initial stages of dating to the commitment to long-term intimacy. Fear of rejection, uncertainty about the future, and the vulnerability inherent in opening up to another person can trigger anxiety. It often disguises itself as excessive thinking, questioning, and even doubt, creating ripples that can disrupt the natural flow of a relationship.

Although the initial emotions of a relationship can be disconcerting, eventually, we will know how to distinguish between pleasant sensations and enjoyment and normal nerves and fear. Falling in love is a universal desire, but for some, the emotions at the beginning of a relationship differ from the typical "butterflies in the stomach."

It is crucial to recognize that anxiety is a common human experience, and its presence in a romantic context does not necessarily mean a failed relationship. Rather, it is an opportunity for growth and understanding, both individually and as a couple. Those who go through anxiety disorders often "fight" these feelings.

"For those suffering from Generalized Anxiety Disorder, in addition to heightened bodily sensations such as a feeling of suffocation and dizziness, there is an added excessive concern about various potential inconveniences. This includes the fear of not being reciprocated by the chosen one, worrying about the possibility of arriving slightly late for an appointment, contemplating what clothing to wear, or fearing an accident while heading to the meeting place. The struggle extends to an inability to properly prioritize these concerns, meaning the intensity of anxiety remains the same, irrespective of the specific causes" (*"Contras"*, 2017).

These individuals perceive that the bodily sensations of falling in love can coincide with those intensified by disorders such as panic, social anxiety, social phobia, and generalized anxiety disorders. To better understand what love is all about, we anxious people must focus on those things that are good for us. Whatever relaxes us.

Dating and Intimacy

In the fascinating world of dating and intimacy, emotions flow like undercurrents, sometimes gentle and warm, other times turbulent and challenging. This journey involves more than just encounters; it is a profound exploration of human connection, where vulnerability, trust, and shared experiences intertwine to create a unique tapestry of relationships. We are talking about a complex interaction.

Within that complexity is anxiety. A partner in this dance who can take on different masks: fear of rejection, uncertainty about the future, and the vulnerability inherent in opening up to someone else. Even the fear of repeating past mistakes. However, it is crucial to understand that anxiety is not an innate enemy but rather a manifestation of our shared humanity. It can be a driving force for personal growth and mutual understanding if approached with empathy and wisdom. The secret is knowing how to handle it.

Well channeled, anxiety becomes a catalyst for individual and collective growth. It can prompt us to question our own perceptions, better understand our deepest emotional needs, and cultivate patience and understanding toward our partner. When approached with respect and openness, anxiety transforms from a disconcerting shadow into a valuable tool.

To manage anxiety, we will see later some practical techniques that you can incorporate into your daily routine and thus change the wiring with which you often deal with relationships. As I said, it is a very personal area. Everyone knows what their strengths are and where they still need to do their homework.

Dealing with Anxiety in Love (Yours and Others)

Navigating anxiety within a romantic relationship requires a thoughtful and proactive approach, encompassing strategies that cater to both your own anxieties and those of your partner. Let's delve deeper into these strategies.

Open Communication: Establishing open and honest communication serves as the cornerstone of dealing with anxiety in a relationship. Create a safe space where both partners feel comfortable expressing their fears, concerns, and vulnerabilities. Initiating conversations about individual anxieties can pave the way for mutual understanding and empathy. This open dialogue fosters emotional intimacy and allows partners to navigate challenges together.

Building Trust: Trust forms the bedrock of any successful relationship, especially when anxiety is a factor. Consistent actions that reflect reliability, honesty, and commitment contribute to building and maintaining trust. Demonstrating transparency and dependability helps alleviate fears and insecurities, creating a foundation upon which the relationship can thrive. Trust-building exercises and shared experiences can further strengthen the emotional bond between partners.

Willingness to Understand: Relationship anxiety often demands a willingness to understand and empathize with each other's perspectives. This involves actively listening, acknowledging differences, and adapting to the unique needs of both partners. The willingness to seek support, whether through professional counseling or relying on a support network, is crucial. By embracing a growth mindset, both individually and collectively, partners can transform relationship challenges into opportunities for personal and shared development.

Commitment to Growth: Acknowledging that personal and shared growth is an ongoing process is vital in managing anxiety within a relationship. Partners should commit to continuous learning, adapting to every evolving circumstance, and addressing challenges collaboratively.

This commitment fosters resilience as both individuals work towards becoming the best versions of themselves, contributing to the overall strength and longevity of the relationship.

Mindfulness and Self-Care: Incorporating mindfulness practices and self-care routines into daily life can significantly impact anxiety levels. Encourage each other to engage in activities that promote relaxation and self-reflection. This might include meditation, exercise, or simply taking moments of solitude to recharge.

Family and Friendships

The connection between family relationships and anxiety is a fundamental aspect of the human experience. The family, as a support network, plays a significant role in both the prevention and management of anxiety. By strengthening family ties, you can create an environment conducive to addressing anxiety, both your own and that of others.

In a strong family environment, people can find the support they need to face and overcome anxiety-inducing challenges. The emotional support and understanding that comes from family can act as a buffer against the stresses of daily life. Open and honest communication in the family creates a space where concerns can be shared and addressed collaboratively.

In some cases, anxiety can run in families, and understanding your family history can be crucial to understanding and managing this aspect of mental health. Family dynamics, shared experiences, and genetics can influence predisposition to anxiety. Addressing these factors from a family perspective can contribute to a more complete understanding and the implementation of effective strategies.

Additionally, the family also plays an essential role in supporting those members who experience anxiety. Empathy, patience, and unconditional love are key elements that can help relieve emotional stress. The family can be a safe haven where anxious people feel understood and accepted, which in turn can have a positive impact on anxiety management.

It is important to note that although family can be a valuable source of support, it is also essential to recognize when professional help is needed. Anxiety sometimes requires specialized intervention, and seeking guidance from mental health professionals can be instrumental in understanding and addressing these challenges.

Strengthening Bonds with Loved Ones

In the digital age, where social networks and virtual communication are predominant, it is essential to recognize and value face-to-face interactions. Time shared in person provides a deeper connection, allowing for the interpretation of non-verbal cues, the sharing of experiences, and the creation of meaningful memories.

To strengthen family ties, it is imperative to prioritize quality time. Whether through shared meals, family outings, or deep conversations, these moments contribute to deeper mutual understanding and lasting appreciation.

Honest communication is the cornerstone of strong relationships. Frank expressions of thoughts, feelings, and concerns foster understanding and facilitate conflict resolution. Nonjudgmental listening promotes empathy and demonstrates a willingness to support and validate the experiences of loved ones.

Showing gratitude through small gestures also plays a crucial role. Expressing gratitude, offering help when needed, or simply being present in times of difficulty demonstrates deep commitment to those we value.

When addressing anxiety in the family context, here are three practical tips to strengthen bonds:

- **Encourage open communication about anxiety:** Creating a space where family members feel safe to talk about anxiety is essential. Encouraging open communication helps understand individual challenges and allows collaboration in finding solutions.

- **Incorporate relaxing family activities:** Introducing activities that promote relaxation and well-being can be beneficial. Whether practicing meditation together, engaging in outdoor activities, or simply spending time on relaxing hobbies, these activities can help reduce stress and strengthen family bonds.

- **Seek joint professional support:** If anxiety affects multiple family members, considering seeking joint professional support may be a valuable option. Family therapy can provide tools and strategies that benefit everyone, strengthening the family unit and addressing individual concerns.

Balancing your Social Connections

Balancing social connections is a delicate art in the modern world, where digital communication, work commitments, and personal responsibilities often compete for our time and attention. Every day, the experiences we live leave their mark on us, affecting us in various ways. By recognizing that these experiences come not only from our own experiences but also from those of those who share life with us, we understand that our social and emotional ties make us vulnerable. Striking the right balance between maintaining social connections and managing individual well-being is crucial for a full and harmonious life, although particularly challenging with anxiety.

- Nowadays, it is easy to find ourselves immersed in virtual interactions, from social networks to instant messaging. While these platforms provide convenient ways to stay in touch, they can sometimes lead to a feeling of disconnection from the real world. Achieving balance involves being aware of the quality of social interactions and not just their quantity.

- At the same time, it is essential to establish healthy boundaries. Overcommitting yourself to social obligations can lead to burnout and stress. Learning to say no when necessary, prioritizing self-care, and respecting personal time are essential components of achieving balance. This not only preserves well-being but also ensures that social interactions remain enjoyable and meaningful.

- When a person faces situations that push their defense mechanisms to the limit, such as high levels of anxiety or unjustified fears, it is difficult to contain what is happening and isolate them from the rest of the family unit. The negative effects of this situation are felt by everyone.

- For those who experience anxiety, it is common to feel that their environment does not understand them despite the closeness that living as a family implies. This feeling creates an expanded cycle as other members begin to experience the effects of overwhelming anxiety. Mothers, fathers, children, and siblings: We are all exposed to what happens in our family, and how we deal with this can determine many things on an individual level. It is a circle in which what affects one affects others and vice versa (CEPFAMI, 2024).

- Quality often trumps quantity when it comes to social connections. Nurturing a few deep, meaningful relationships can be more satisfying than spreading yourself too thin among numerous superficial connections. Investing time and energy in relationships that bring genuine joy, support, and understanding improves overall life satisfaction.

- Balancing social connections also means recognizing the changing dynamics of relationships. As life evolves, so do our social circles. Some connections may fade naturally while new ones emerge. Accepting these changes with adaptability and an open heart allows for continued growth and enrichment of social connections.

- In the workplace, striking a balance between professional and social interactions is equally important. Establishing positive relationships with colleagues contributes to a healthy work environment, fostering collaboration and a sense of camaraderie. However, it is essential to set boundaries to prevent work-related stress from invading your personal life.

In this chapter, we have explored the intricate path of navigating anxiety to build meaningful relationships. Reflection on the importance of building genuine connections has been the common thread, highlighting the need for authenticity and emotional health in our interactions. In these pages, we have weighed the delicate task of balancing family life with anxiety, recognizing that our individual experiences impact the entire circle of relationships.

Throughout the book, we have discussed the fundamental idea that profound change begins within oneself. The practical tools we offer in these pages can be powerful, but their real impact depends on the mindset with which we approach them. Forging a positive and open mindset is the first step toward effectively incorporating practical strategies into our daily lives.

Looking back, it highlights the need to manage and control anxiety, especially in the context of romantic relationships and dating. Understanding how anxiety can influence our romantic interactions becomes a crucial skill for cultivating healthy, long-lasting bonds.

I always invite my readers to not just read these words but internalize and truly connect with the strategies and exercises presented. This book is not just a compendium of theories; it invites you to maintain a positive attitude, and being open to change is essential. I invite you to reflect on the tools that resonate most deeply with you and make an active commitment to incorporating them into your lives.

As we enter the next stage of our journey, we delve into the fascinating and transformative dimension of empathy. This powerful component stands as the cornerstone of building meaningful relationships. In these chapters, we will venture beyond the surface of human interactions, addressing the limits that communication sometimes encounters and exploring how empathy can unlock the doors to deeper understanding.

So far, we have reflected on the importance of forging authentic connections and have explored strategies for managing anxiety in various spheres of our lives. However, we understand that the true essence of human relationships goes beyond words and visible actions. This is where empathy comes into play, an act of putting yourself in another's shoes, of understanding not only what is being said but also what is being felt.

On this journey toward a more enriching and connected life, we will address the challenges of communication and how empathy can be a master key to overcoming those obstacles. We will explore how the ability to tune into the emotions and perspectives of others can open previously closed doors, creating bridges to deeper understanding and a stronger social fabric.

Empathy connects us with others more authentically and gives us the ability to see beyond appearances. As we venture into this new territory, we challenge you to prepare for a shift in perspective, to make room for vulnerability, and to explore how empathy can radically transform the way we relate to the world around us.

Chapter 5:

Empathic Communication 101

Empathy, the ability to understand and share the feelings of others, emerges as the axis in the field of meaningful relationships. As anxiety often introduces complexities and nuances into interpersonal dynamics, fostering and applying empathy becomes paramount. It serves as a guiding force that allows people to navigate the intricate landscapes of emotions, perspectives, and experiences.

This chapter unfolds as a deep exploration of empathy, an indispensable asset that transcends the challenges posed by anxiety. Recognizing that empathy is the cornerstone, this chapter delves into the transformative power it has to foster connections that resist and transcend the impact of anxiety.

When anxiety participates in daily dynamics, empathy becomes a bridge that connects people on a deeper and more authentic level. It allows those experiencing anxiety to feel truly understood, creating a safe space within relationships. At the same time, it equips those who offer empathy with the insight and compassion necessary to support their loved ones through the challenges that anxiety can pose.

During this chapter, we will see how empathy acts as a counterforce to the isolating nature of anxiety. It encourages open dialogue where people can express their fears, concerns, and vulnerabilities without fear of being judged. In doing so, empathy becomes a catalyst for breaking down the barriers that anxiety can erect, fostering an environment of trust and mutual understanding.

As readers delve deeper into the exploration of empathy, the chapter emphasizes its role not only in understanding others but also in cultivating self-compassion. By extending empathy inward, people facing anxiety can develop a kinder, nurturing relationship with themselves, fostering resilience and a sense of inner security.

Additionally, the chapter delves into practical strategies for honing empathic skills and provides practical insights into active listening, perspective-taking, and fostering emotional intelligence, all crucial components of the empathic toolkit. These skills, when exercised intentionally, have the potential to transform relationships, creating a tapestry woven of threads of understanding, support, and connection. In this way, we are ready to embrace empathy so that it becomes a guiding light that paves the way for resilient, authentic, and deeply enriching relationships, even in the face of anxiety.

The Power of Empathy

Empathy, often described as the ability to understand and share the feelings of others, is the cornerstone of effective communication. It is a powerful force that transcends mere words, forging connections that are not only meaningful but transformative. In essence, empathy involves not only recognizing the emotions of others but also genuinely sharing their experiences, creating a bridge of understanding that strengthens interpersonal relationships.

Understanding and sharing the feelings of others is the essence of empathy. It goes beyond sympathy and delves into a realm where individuals actively interact with the emotional landscape of those around them. This shared emotional experience lays the foundation for authentic connections as it fosters a deep sense of validation and recognition.

In the context of effective communication, empathy serves as a key piece. When people feel understood and recognized, communication channels open more, allowing for more honest and transparent exchanges. By recognizing and sharing emotions, people create an environment where trust can flourish, forming the foundation for fruitful relationships.

Empathy plays a critical role in building stronger connections. It is a unifying force that transcends differences, fostering a sense of camaraderie and shared humanity. When people feel heard and understood, relationships deepen, and the bonds formed become more resilient. Whether in personal or professional settings, empathy acts as a catalyst for collaboration, teamwork, and mutual support.

An integral aspect of empathic communication is building a skill that goes beyond hearing words to truly understanding the emotions and intentions behind them. This means being fully present in a conversation, suspending judgment, and offering genuine feedback.

Active Listening Techniques

Active listening is a fundamental skill that goes beyond simply hearing words; It involves fully engaging with the speaker and understanding the emotions and intentions behind their message. Mastering active listening techniques improves communication, fosters understanding, and strengthens relationships. Below are some key techniques to become an effective active listener:

Paraphrasing:

What it entails: Rephrase the speaker's message in your own words.

Why it's important: Paraphrasing confirms that you have correctly understood the speaker's message and provides an opportunity to clarify it.

Example: "If I understood correctly, you are saying that..."

Summarizing:

What it entails: Provide a concise overview of the key points discussed.

Why it's important: Summarizing helps distill the main ideas and ensure alignment between both parties.

Example: "So, to summarize, the main topics we have discussed are..."

Reflecting feelings:

What it entails: Recognize and validate the emotions expressed by the speaker.

Why it's important: Reflecting feelings demonstrates empathy and shows that you recognize the emotional aspect of the conversation.

Example: "You seem to be frustrated because..."

Open questions:

What it entails: Encourage the speaker to share more by asking questions that require more than a simple yes or no answer.

Why it's important: Open-ended questions promote a deeper exploration of thoughts and feelings.

Example: "Can you tell me more about how you feel about...?"

Clarifying:

What it entails: Look for additional information or details to ensure complete understanding.

Why it's important: Clarification prevents misunderstandings and shows your commitment to grasping the finer points of the conversation.

Example: "I want to make sure I understand correctly; could you clarify your point about..."

Non-verbal cues:

What it entails: Using body language, such as maintaining eye contact and nodding, to convey attention.

Why it's important: Nonverbal cues reinforce your engagement and show that you are fully present in the conversation.

Example: Making eye contact, nodding your head, or leaning forward slightly.

Avoid interrupting:

What it entails: Allowing the speaker to express himself without interruption.

Why it's important: Avoiding interruptions shows respect for the speaker's perspective and allows for a more fluid and open exchange.

Example: Wait for a pause before responding to the speaker.

Tester Comments:

What it entails: Offer constructive comments or statements to indicate your understanding.

Why it's important: Feedback assures the speaker that their message has been received and encourages continued communication.

Example: "I appreciate your perspective on this and it helps me understand your point of view."

Utilizing these strategies proves invaluable when engaging with colleagues in a professional setting, especially in a supervisory role. They have the potential to significantly enhance the overall workplace atmosphere.

Additionally, these approaches can be beneficial when dealing with someone experiencing GAD who tends to be excessively concerned about various aspects of life and harbors constant fears of impending negativity. This individual may often struggle to embrace life to the fullest.

Expressing Yourself When Dealing With Anxiety

Living with or interacting with others who have anxiety can be a complex journey, and one of the key components of navigating this path is expressing yourself effectively. The ability to articulate feelings and needs is not only therapeutic but also essential for gaining the support of others and fostering a sense of empowerment. In this section, we explore the nuances of expressing yourself while dealing with anxiety, recognizing its importance in promoting understanding and creating an environment conducive to open communication.

First of all, it is essential to recognize and accept one's own feelings. Anxiety is a valid and common human experience, and giving yourself permission to feel without judgment is the critical step to effective expression. Identifying and articulating specific emotions is the next stage, which allows people to communicate their internal experiences more clearly.

Selecting an appropriate time and environment becomes essential when expressing feelings of anxiety. A calm and comfortable environment fosters a safe space for open communication. Using "I" statements is another crucial aspect, squaring thoughts to express personal feelings without attributing blame. This approach encourages non-confrontational dialogue, promoting understanding between people.

Sharing specific examples of situations that trigger anxiety provides context and depth to the expression. Concrete instances allow others to understand experiences more fully, facilitating meaningful discussion and support. Furthermore, expressing needs clearly is essential. Communicating what one needs, whether it's understanding, reassurance, or practical assistance, sets the stage for constructive engagement.

Expression does not always have to be verbal; People can employ various communication methods that align with their comfort and authenticity. Writing in a journal, participating in artistic activities, or using technology are alternative channels to transmit emotions. Choosing the medium that resonates most deeply can enhance the effectiveness of expression.

Fostering an environment that encourages two-way communication is integral. Creating a space where people feel comfortable expressing their thoughts and feelings while being open to the perspectives of others helps create an atmosphere of support and understanding.

Assertiveness vs. Aggressiveness

Effective communication is the cornerstone of healthy relationships, and the way people express their thoughts and feelings plays a crucial role in promoting mutual understanding and respect. Two communication styles that frequently emerge are assertiveness and aggressiveness. Although both involve the expression of needs and opinions, their approaches and consequences differ substantially in interpersonal dynamics.

Assertiveness is characterized by a clear and direct expression of thoughts, feelings, and needs, always respecting the rights and opinions of others. It involves the ability to defend oneself without undermining the rights of others, promoting honesty, and establishing solid foundations for healthy relationships.

In contrast, aggressiveness manifests itself with forcefulness, dominance, and disregard for the feelings and opinions of others. Those who adopt an aggressive style are prone to putting their needs first, sometimes using intimidating or critical tactics, creating a hostile environment that undermines trust and damages relationships.

Aggressive communication seeks to gain at the expense of others, using accusatory statements and a confrontational tone. This can lead to conflict, resentment, and decreased effectiveness in communication.

I personally experienced the difference between these styles in a specific situation. On one occasion, I consciously opted for assertiveness rather than aggressiveness when addressing a misunderstanding at work. Instead of blaming others and using a confrontational tone, I expressed my concerns clearly and respectfully, using "I" instead of "you." This approach resulted in more effective communication, resolving the problem constructively and preserving harmony in the work environment.

This personal experience underscores the importance of consciously choosing an assertive approach to communication to build healthy relationships and resolve conflicts effectively. Assertiveness not only promotes mutual understanding but also preserves the integrity of human connections, building bridges instead of barriers.

Achieving Balance

The essence of effective communication lies in the ability to find a balance between assertiveness and aggressiveness. By offering people the opportunity to express themselves authentically while respecting the rights of others, assertiveness lays the foundation for open and constructive dialogue. This approach involves more than simply expressing opinions; it's about setting clear boundaries, communicating needs effectively, and standing up for yourself without undermining the rights and perspectives of those around you.

To achieve this balance, it is essential to cultivate self-awareness, practice active listening, and exercise empathy. Self-awareness involves reflecting on our own communication style and identifying areas where we could improve assertiveness and reduce aggressive behaviors. Active listening, on the other hand, allows us to understand the needs and concerns of others, facilitating a more enriching and respectful exchange.

Cultivating assertiveness and mitigating tendencies toward aggression requires a conscious and practical approach. Here, I present three practical strategies that readers can incorporate into their daily lives to strengthen their communication.

Practice Clear and Direct Communication

In cultivating effective communication, clarity and directness form the bedrock. Rather than relying on vague or ambiguous expressions, make a conscious effort to be clear and direct in your communication. Clearly articulate your thoughts and needs, using first-person statements to convey your perspective without attributing blame to others. This approach not only enhances your assertiveness but also ensures that your message is received and understood accurately. The power of clear and direct communication lies in its ability to minimize misunderstandings, paving the way for more constructive interactions and relationships.

Use Breathing and Calming Techniques

When faced with moments of tension, integrating breathing and calming techniques becomes a valuable tool for navigating challenging situations. Instead of succumbing to impulsive or aggressive reactions, take a deliberate pause. Inhale deeply, count to ten before responding and allow this moment of reprieve to gain the mental clarity needed for assertive communication. These techniques serve as a practical means to manage heightened emotions, fostering a composed and collected meaning.

Promote a Space for Open Dialogue

Building a culture of assertiveness involves promoting a space for open and respectful dialogue. Cultivate an environment that encourages individuals to express their opinions and feelings honestly. Acknowledge and validate diverse perspectives, recognizing that each person brings a unique viewpoint to the table. This inclusive approach to communication contributes to a collaborative and understanding atmosphere where diverse voices are heard and respected.

Communicating Boundaries

The complexities of social communication become particularly nuanced when it comes to dealing with anxiety, whether it's your own or someone else's. An aspect that is extremely important in these situations is the effective communication of limits. Understanding how to set and communicate boundaries becomes a vital skill, fostering an environment of respect, support, and overall well-being.

Assertiveness, the ability to clearly express our needs, thoughts, and emotions, plays a crucial role in establishing communication boundaries. It provides clarity in communication, promoting mutual respect by expressing boundaries in a firm but thoughtful manner. It acts as a shield against manipulation, protecting autonomy and strengthening self-esteem by affirming our values.

Additionally, it fosters an environment conducive to personal and relational growth, encouraging mutual understanding and collaborative adjustments. In short, assertiveness becomes a valuable tool for building authentic connections based on respect and mutual understanding.

Communicating your own limits: When struggling with anxiety, articulating personal boundaries becomes essential to maintaining emotional balance. It involves clearly expressing what you need in terms of space, time, and support. Honesty is key, and using "I" statements can be a powerful way to communicate without blaming. For example, stating, "I need some time alone right now to manage my anxiety," sets a clear boundary without accusing others of causing distress.

It is crucial to understand that your boundaries may evolve, and it is perfectly acceptable to communicate these changes as your needs change. Regular check-ins with yourself can help you identify when adjustments are necessary, ensuring that those around you are aware of your current limits.

Respect the boundaries of others: On the other hand, it is equally important to understand and respect the boundaries of other people who may be dealing with anxiety. This involves actively listening and watching for signs that indicate when someone might need space or support. It is essential to avoid intruding or pressuring, allowing people to express their needs when they are ready.

Recognizing and validating the boundaries set by others helps create a supportive environment. Instead of making assumptions, consider asking open-ended questions like, "Is there anything I can do to support you right now?" This shows your willingness to respect their boundaries while also offering assistance if needed.

Creating a safe communication space: Creating a safe communication space is a foundational element in managing relationships, particularly when anxiety is in the equation. This goes beyond mere physical surroundings; it encompasses the emotional and psychological atmosphere where individuals can express themselves authentically and without apprehension.

In the context of anxiety, where vulnerability often intertwines with communication, establishing a safe space becomes paramount. It involves consciously cultivating an environment where people feel not only heard but also understood and supported.

Flexibility and adaptability: Anxiety can be unpredictable, and flexibility is crucial when it comes to boundaries. Recognize that some days may require different levels of support or solitude. Flexibility involves understanding that boundaries may need to change based on the ebb and flow of anxiety levels.

In practical terms, this might mean communicating openly with trusted individuals about shifting needs and expectations. It involves being attuned to one's emotional state and, when necessary, expressing the requirement for different levels of support or solitude. Flexibility empowers individuals to prioritize self-care without feeling confined to rigid boundaries that might not serve their well-being in every circumstance.

Navigating Social Dynamics

Social dynamics can become challenging terrain to navigate when anxiety is a companion. For many, myself included, dealing with anxiety in social situations has been a journey of self-discovery and adaptation. Below is a look at this personal exploration and the strategies employed to navigate social dynamics with a touch of anxiety.

Accepting vulnerability is a powerful antidote to anxiety, as it counteracts the fear of judgment or scrutiny. Recognizing and accepting that it is okay to feel anxious in social settings opens the door to self-compassion, reminding us that vulnerability is not a weakness but a shared human experience.

Navigating social dynamics requires a strategic approach to exposure. Gradual exposure to social situations allows acclimatization to anxiety triggers. Starting with smaller, more manageable environments and progressively moving to more challenging environments allows people to develop resilience over time.

During my teenage years, dealing with social dynamics was an overwhelming challenge due to my constant struggle with anxiety. Every social interaction seemed to be an internal battle between the desire to connect with others and the incessant worry about how it would be perceived. Social gatherings became tension-filled events, and the anticipation of social situations was overshadowed by the fear of not fitting in.

At that stage, my social anxiety dictated my interactions. Constant self-criticism and fear of rejection were lingering shadows that clouded any possibility of fully enjoying the company of others. It was a period in which I sadly walked away from many valuable opportunities for connection and personal growth.

Over time, and into adulthood, I decided to address my social anxiety head-on. As I mentioned at the beginning of the book: face your fears. I began a process of self-exploration and learning that involved understanding the roots of my fears and developing effective strategies to deal with them. One of the key aspects was incorporating healthy communication habits.

I learned to be more aware of my automatic thoughts and challenge the negative beliefs ingrained in my mind. The practice of self-acceptance and compassion for myself became fundamental pillars in overcoming the barrier of social anxiety. I began to recognize that it's okay to be imperfect and that social interactions don't need to be perfect.

Assertive communication was a game changer. Instead of letting anxiety dictate my participation in conversations, I began to express my thoughts and feelings honestly and respectfully. Setting clear boundaries and openly sharing my concerns allowed me to feel more in control of social situations.

I understood that setting realistic expectations is crucial to navigating social dynamics. Accepting that not every interaction will be perfect or anxiety-free is liberating. Accepting imperfections and understanding that socializing is a learning process relieves the pressure of meeting unrealistic standards.

In this chapter, we have explored the complexities of empathy and the dynamics of social communication in the context of anxiety. Diving into the intersection of these two forces means we have discovered empathy as a fundamental bridge to understanding others—also a powerful tool to manage anxiety in our interactions.

Amid the emotional turbulence that anxiety can generate, empathy stands as a beacon, guiding us toward a deeper understanding of ourselves and those around us. We have learned that by cultivating empathy, we create a space where authentic connections flourish, providing respite from the emotional turmoil that anxiety can unleash.

It is essential to remember that on this journey towards improving our social communication skills and managing anxiety, we must remain focused on the goal and resilient in the face of challenges. Each step, however small, brings us closer to a more skilled and compassionate version of ourselves.

In our next chapter, we'll dive into the practical realm with "Strategies to Overcome Social Challenges." Here, we will focus on tangible tools and practical techniques designed to address head-on the challenges and anxieties inherent to social interactions. Recognizing that there are no magic solutions or easy shortcuts, we will explore strategies that require effort and dedication but that promise to illuminate our path to more effective communication and richer relationships.

On this journey of self-exploration and growth, let us remember that every effort invested carries with it the possibility of significant transformation. There is no evolution without sacrifice or improvement without dedication. Let us continue to move forward with the conviction that, through continuous effort, we can shape and improve our most authentic version and connect with others.

Chapter 6:

Strategies for Overcoming Social Challenges

The essence of human existence is intrinsically linked to society, where the complexities inherent in social interaction pose challenges that can leave significant imprints on our mental and emotional well-being. This chapter dives into the complexities of these social challenges, exploring strategies that not only address these complexities but also seek to empower people, providing them with the tools necessary to navigate these waters with confidence and resilience.

Overcoming social challenges is revealed to be a multifaceted endeavor that requires a careful combination of self-awareness, effective communication skills, empathy, and a continuous commitment to learning. Implementing these strategies not only allows individuals to confidently navigate the complexities of social interactions but also empowers them to forge deeper connections and actively contribute to the creation of positive and supportive social environments.

Acceptance of personal growth emerges as a fundamental pillar in this journey, where a deep understanding of oneself acts as the foundation to address social challenges with clarity and authenticity. Maintaining an open mindset becomes a guiding beacon, allowing individuals to adapt to the diversity of social experiences and embrace the constant evolution that arises from interaction with others.

In the infinite web of human connections, these strategies not only act as practical tools but also as a moral compass that guides individuals toward more satisfying and enriching social interactions. We must think of perfecting communication skills as a key element in this journey since the ability to express thoughts and emotions clearly and effectively establishes the foundation for a deeper connection with others.

Empathy, as a cornerstone of meaningful connections, is consciously cultivated, allowing individuals to understand and share the feelings of others. This skill not only enriches relationships but also contributes to the creation of a social environment in which diversity of perspectives is valued and respected.

Social Events Survival Guide

The path to overcoming social challenges begins with recognizing personal strengths, weaknesses, and triggers that lay the foundation for approaching social situations with a clear mindset. Authenticity flourishes when people have a deep understanding of themselves, fostering genuine connections with others.

In this context, communication is the key to successful social interactions. Skills such as active listening, assertiveness, and non-verbal communication allow people to express thoughts and emotions clearly. Practicing open and honest communication fosters understanding and minimizes the risk of misunderstanding.

We're diving into the Social Event Survival Guide, your go-to manual for acing social gatherings without breaking a sweat.

Social Gatherings Mentality

Let's delve into the notion of navigating social events as a deliberate and conscious task. Social gatherings, as is acknowledged, can indeed feel like venturing into uncharted territories. However, maintaining a sense of agency in such situations is paramount.

The initial step involves freeing yourself from the self-imposed burden of assuming the central role in the festivities. Embracing the understanding that authenticity, with all its idiosyncrasies and occasional discomforts, is not only acceptable but commendable lays the foundation for more genuine engagement in social settings.

Fundamentally, it is imperative to recognize that every social interaction does not need to be metamorphosed into a theatrical performance or an intellectually charged TED talk. True authenticity, marked by sincere expressions, active listening, and insightful articulation of thoughts, imparts a unique richness to social gatherings. The tapestry of diversity within personalities weaves a vibrant fabric, and appreciating this process is key to deriving satisfaction from these experiences.

In cases where a conversation becomes energetically draining, there is no need to succumb to a state of panic. Excusing yourself gracefully, taking a brief respite, and finding a new group to interact with exemplifies not only a pragmatic approach but also underscores the adaptability inherent in social experience. This dynamic ability to navigate diverse social contexts underscores the fluidity of interpersonal connections.

Mastery of social events depends on recognition of your strengths, acceptance of authenticity, and appreciation of the diverse tapestry of personalities within the social sphere. Beyond the surface level, these experiences offer an opportunity for personal growth, fostering connections that extend beyond the immediate boundaries of any meeting.

I often mention having "seating anxiety" because I feel uneasy attending events with designated seating. The thought of uncertain conversations and the potential struggle to keep them engaging leaves me concerned. Being in situations that make me uncomfortable and drain my energy isn't enjoyable. However, with time, I've improved in handling these moments and can now participate in conversations more comfortably.

Coping With Overstimulation

Now, we address the topic of overstimulation, a challenging facet that can arise unexpectedly during social events. Although this phenomenon may cause surprise, it should not cause apprehension. Let's equip ourselves with effective strategies to deal with sensory overload.

First, it is wise to identify a quiet refuge. Finding a serene space, taking a breath, and recharging are essential actions to preserve mental health. If the growing crowd threatens to overwhelm the senses, consider using earplugs as a discreet but effective tactic. This resource, in my opinion, can positively alter the dynamics of the environment.

When trivial interactions begin to put overwhelming pressure on the introverted spirit, I suggest focusing on the quality, rather than the quantity, of the interactions. Making deeper connections with one or two people can transform your perception of the sea of faces into something more manageable and meaningful.

It is essential not to overlook the importance of establishing time limits. Implementing a planned exit strategy, backed by a reasonable excuse, enables a graceful exit when social fatigue sets in. In this context, preserving mental health emerges as an undisputed priority.

The essence of surviving and thriving at social events goes beyond mere interaction; It involves a deep understanding and acceptance of the uniqueness inherent in each individual. In this complex social fabric, recognizing and valuing differences becomes the basis of an enriching experience. Each person brings a unique perspective, a singular set of experiences, and qualities that contribute to the richness of the social encounter.

Taking strategic pauses emerges as a wise practice on this social journey. By recognizing the importance of taking care of our emotional well-being, we are given the power to consciously measure our participation. These breaks not only allow us to recharge but also offer moments of reflection, fostering a more authentic connection with ourselves and those around us.

Social anxiety can be a formidable obstacle in social interactions. Overcoming it requires gradual exposure to social situations, along with relaxation techniques and positive self-talk. Unrealistic expectations often sow the seeds of disappointment and frustration in social interactions. Realism involves recognizing that not all interactions will be perfect and appreciating the diversity of communication styles. Accepting imperfections relieves unnecessary stress in social encounters.

The discernment to withdraw gracefully when the situation requires it is an invaluable virtue. Knowing how to identify personal boundaries and recognize when it is time to end an interaction reflects a sophisticated social skill. Leaving gracefully does not imply rejection or disinterest but rather a show of respect for one's own well-being and that of others.

Therefore, this vast world of interactions awaits like a vacation to be discovered, and you, with your distinctive individualities, take the place of distinguished guest. In this diverse social scenario, openness to new experiences and the willingness to learn from the singularities of those around us become the pillars of a meaningful social experience. Thus, we celebrate not only the interaction itself but also the opportunity for personal and collective growth that each social encounter offers.

Handling Criticism and Rejection

Handling criticism and rejection in the context of anxiety and social gatherings can be a daunting challenge, but developing coping strategies and a resilient mindset can make these situations more manageable.

Remember, dealing with criticism and rejection is a skill that develops with practice. Fostering self-compassion, maintaining realistic expectations, and learning from experiences allow you to develop resilience in social settings and minimize the impact of anxiety associated with these challenges.

Here's a guide on how to deal with criticism and rejection with grace and self-compassion:

Change your perspective: Instead of viewing criticism and rejection as personal attacks, consider them opportunities for growth. Understand that everyone encounters moments of critique, and these instances do not define your overall value. Embrace feedback as a valuable tool for self-improvement rather than a reflection of inadequacy.

Practice self-compassion: Acknowledge that anxiety can intensify the emotional impact of criticism and rejection. Extend kindness to yourself, treating your inner dialogue with the same compassion you would offer a friend in similar circumstances. Recognize and celebrate your efforts and progress, fostering a positive and supportive self-narrative.

Separate your value from the situation: Remind yourself that your worth as an individual is not solely determined by a single meeting or social interaction. Criticism or rejection within a specific context does not define your overall value or abilities. Cultivate a sense of self-worth independent of situational outcomes.

Set realistic expectations: Acknowledge that not every social interaction will unfold perfectly, and not every individual will respond positively. Setting realistic expectations helps manage potential disappointment and allows room for personal growth. Understand that setbacks are inherent in the learning process.

Look for constructive feedback: When faced with criticism, strive to discern constructive feedback from unwarranted negativity. Constructive criticism provides specific areas for improvement, and accepting it can pave the way for personal development. Embrace feedback as a valuable resource for refining your skills and approaches.

Engage in positive self-talk: Counter negative thoughts associated with criticism or rejection by incorporating positive affirmations into your inner dialogue. Challenge irrational beliefs and replace them with more balanced and realistic perspectives. Positive self-talk contributes to building resilience and fostering a healthier mindset.

Learn from rejections: Treat rejections as opportunities for learning and growth. Objectively analyze the situation, identify areas for potential improvement, and use feedback to refine your social skills. Each rejection can serve as a stepping stone toward personal development and increased resilience.

Consider professional help: If criticism and rejection consistently trigger overwhelming anxiety, consider seeking professional help, such as therapy. A mental health professional can provide valuable tools and strategies to manage and overcome these challenges, fostering emotional well-being.

Practice social skills: Enhance your social skills through deliberate practice. Start with low-pressure social situations and gradually expose yourself to larger gatherings. This incremental approach allows you to build confidence and trust in your abilities over time, ultimately contributing to improved social interactions.

The Impact of Poorly Managed Social Situations

The manner in which individuals navigate and handle social situations can exert profound psychological impacts, given the pivotal role that social interactions play in shaping mental health and emotional well-being. The consequences of poor handling of social situations extend across various dimensions, encompassing cognitive, emotional, and behavioral aspects of an individual's psychological landscape.

Over time, the cumulative effects of poor social handling can contribute to more severe mental health issues. Chronic social stressors and negative interpersonal experiences may increase the risk of developing anxiety disorders, depression, and other mental health conditions. The lack of effective coping strategies and social support exacerbates the challenges, creating a complex interplay between social difficulties and mental well-being.

Here are some of the possible psychological effects:

Low self-esteem

Negative experiences in social situations can undermine self-esteem. The constant perception of poor performance or rejection can lead to a negative self-image and contribute to feelings of not being worthy or accepted.

Social isolation

Repeated mishandling of social interactions can lead to isolation. People may avoid social situations to avoid facing associated distress, which in turn limits opportunities for social connection and support.

Depression

Lack of effective social skills and negative experiences can contribute to the development of depression. Loneliness, isolation, and lack of connection can negatively impact mood and mental health.

Chronic stress

Poorly managed social situations can generate chronic stress. A constant fear of social interactions can trigger stress responses that, over time, can contribute to physical and mental health problems.

Distorted perception of relationships

Lack of social skills can lead to a distorted perception of relationships. People can misinterpret social cues, contributing to misunderstandings and conflicts, which affect the quality of relationships.

Generalized insecurity

Negative experiences in social situations can contribute to a general feeling of insecurity. This can manifest itself in various areas of life, affecting decision-making, the expression of opinions, and the search for new experiences.

It is important to note that these impacts can vary in intensity depending on the frequency and severity of poorly managed social situations, as well as the individual's willingness to address and learn from these experiences. In many cases, seeking psychological support, such as therapy, can be beneficial in developing social skills, improving self-esteem, and addressing associated psychological impacts.

Turning Rejection into Growth Opportunities

Embracing rejection as a catalyst for personal growth is a transformative mindset that can lead to resilience and success. Instead of seeing rejection as a dead end, it is an opportunity to learn, redirect, and ultimately improve. Reflect on rejection as part of a learning curve, drawing valuable lessons for personal and professional development.

The emotional resilience cultivated when facing rejection builds strength and adaptability. Adjust expectations realistically, seeking constructive feedback where possible to understand the reasons behind rejection and guide improvement. Use rejection as a driver of personal development, identifying areas to improve skills.

Cultivate a growth mindset, seeing challenges as opportunities for growth and celebrating the courage to face rejection. Be flexible, willing to pivot and adapt strategies, exploring alternative paths. Surround yourself with a support network that encourages you to confront rejection and turn setbacks into opportunities for growth.

This way, every rejection becomes an opportunity to refine your approach, evolve, and become a more resilient and fulfilled version of yourself.

Building Professional Relationships

Building professional relationships with people dealing with anxiety requires a thoughtful and empathetic approach. Anxiety can affect several aspects of a person's life, including their work environment.

Remember that building professional relationships with people facing anxiety requires ongoing effort and commitment to creating an inclusive and supportive work environment. It will be necessary to commit to helping others, prioritizing open communication, empathy, and personalized support. In this way, you will be contributing to a work culture that values the well-being of all its members.

To foster positive connections and support those facing anxiety, consider the following strategies:

Empathy at work: Take the time to understand the unique challenges people with anxiety may face. Show empathy and avoid making assumptions about their abilities. Recognize that anxiety can manifest differently in each person and that their experiences are valid.

Work flexibility: Consider implementing flexible work arrangements, such as adjustable hours or remote work options. Providing a sense of control over your work environment can help alleviate anxiety triggers and contribute to better overall well-being.

Be clear with expectations: Clearly communicate expectations regarding tasks, deadlines, and performance. Ambiguity can be a source of stress for people dealing with anxiety. Providing a roadmap for success can help them navigate their responsibilities more effectively.

Become a real leader: Leadership plays a crucial role in creating a supportive work environment. Encourage leaders to be approachable and understanding. Promote a culture in which seeking help or discussing mental health problems is not stigmatized.

Think about the work environment: Work with people to identify specific accommodations that may be helpful. This could include quiet workspaces, extra breaks, or access to mental health resources. Tailoring support to individual needs can make a significant difference.

Promote a sense of belonging within the team: Inclusive team-building activities can help people feel more connected and supported, reducing feelings of isolation that often accompany anxiety.

Positive Reinforcement: Provide regular, constructive feedback on performance. Positive reinforcement can increase confidence and help people feel more secure in their roles.

Anxiety and Networking

Networking plays a vital role in personal and professional development and offers valuable opportunities for growth, collaboration, and support. When it comes to anxiety, effective networking can provide a supportive framework to overcome challenges and foster a sense of community.

Below are practical tips for starting and nurturing professional relationships, along with guidance on effective communication in the context of networking:

- Start by attending smaller, more intimate meetings or events so you can network. This can help alleviate anxiety associated with large crowds and provide a more comfortable environment for meaningful connections.

- Use professional networking platforms like LinkedIn to connect with peers, industry professionals, and potential mentors. Online interactions can be less intimidating and allow for thoughtful communication at your own pace.

- Become a member of industry-specific organizations or groups. This provides opportunities to attend events, workshops, or webinars where you can connect with like-minded professionals who share common interests.

Networking Communication

Effective communication in the field of networking encompasses both body language and verbal expression. It is crucial to maintain positive body language with eye contact, open gestures, and a posture that conveys confidence. Active listening and clear communication in verbal interactions are equally essential. Developing an effective presentation speech makes it easy to present objectives and skills in a concise and engaging way.

Digital communication also plays a vital role. In online environments, it is essential to maintain professionalism in messages, ensuring they are clear and concise. Digital communication etiquette includes taking care of tone to ensure messages are received positively. Strategically using social networks, participating in relevant conversations, and keeping profiles updated are important tools to strengthen your professional network.

Reciprocity and authenticity are fundamental principles in networking. Offering help and resources, as well as asking for them when needed, contributes to strong, mutually beneficial relationships. Cultivating authentic connections means going beyond the accumulation of contacts, sharing experiences, and valuing diversity of perspectives. It is essential to continually evaluate and adjust your networking strategy to adapt to changing objectives and take advantage of emerging opportunities.

Consistency in networking efforts over time leads to more successful results, highlighting the importance of quality over quantity in professional connections.

Professional Relationships and Anxiety

Professional relationships can be a significant source of growth and opportunity, but for some people, especially those experiencing anxiety, the process of establishing and maintaining connections can be challenging. Aware of their body language, those facing anxiety should strive to maintain eye contact, use welcoming gestures, and adopt a posture that exudes confidence. Positive body language can not only improve the communication experience but also alleviate the tension associated with professional interactions.

It is crucial to clearly articulate career goals and aspirations, as this not only allows others to understand individual interests but can also open the door to valuable information and connections. However, in the context of anxiety, sharing these goals can lead to insecurity. It's important to remember that building relationships takes time, and each interaction should be approached with patience and an open mind.

Digital communication and online networking also play a vital role, and those facing anxiety should pay attention to digital etiquette. Maintaining professionalism in online messages and profiles, as well as crafting clear and concise messages, can help build virtual connections more comfortably and effectively.

Follow up

After initial interactions, follow up with a brief email or message expressing your gratitude for the connection. Reference specific points in your conversation to show attention and interest.

Provide value

Offer assistance or share relevant resources when appropriate. Providing value to your network establishes you as a valuable and supportive connection. This reciprocity strengthens professional relationships.

Attend networking events regularly

Consistency is essential for building relationships. Attend networking events regularly to maintain and expand your network. Familiar faces can make future interactions more comfortable.

This journey toward understanding the social challenges associated with anxiety has been eye-opening. Personally, discovering the strategies that facilitate proper dealing with people who suffer from anxiety has been transformative. Understanding the complexity of the minds of those who face this daily battle has generated in me a deep reflection on the importance of cultivating empathy and adopting practices that strengthen social and professional relationships.

Recognizing that anxiety is not simply an individual obstacle but a shared experience in our society has changed my perspective. The strategies explored are not only presented as tools to alleviate anxiety on an individual basis but also as means to build bridges of understanding and support between people.

It has been essential to apply these strategies in my own life. Thanks to them, I have experienced how open communication and genuine empathy can transform interpersonal dynamics. Understanding the signs of anxiety in others has strengthened my relationships as I have learned to adapt my approach and provide the necessary support in critical moments.

We will now enter a new chapter that will delve into the fascinating territory of well-being in the context of anxiety. Through this journey, we will not only learn about everyday practices that can positively impact our mental health, but we will also reflect on the intrinsic connection between individual well-being and the strength of our personal and professional relationships.

Anxiety, when approached from a holistic perspective, is not only a challenge to overcome individually but an opportunity to cultivate an environment that fosters mutual understanding, respect, and support. I look forward to exploring the transformative power of good habits with you in the next chapter and discovering how they can positively influence our daily lives and contribute to building stronger, more satisfying relationships.

Chapter 7:

Wellness in Anxiety

As we delve deeper into exploring strategies to manage anxiety, I can't help but reflect on the current state of well-being in today's society. Recently, I found myself immersed in the relentless pace of modern life, juggling professional responsibilities, personal commitments, and the ever-present digital demands. The prevailing social atmosphere seemed to prioritize constant productivity over holistic well-being, fostering an environment where anxiety could easily take root.

In the midst of this, I stumbled upon the profound impact of incorporating intentional strategies to manage stress and anxiety into my daily routine. The search for a sense of balance and well-being led me to experiment with mindfulness practices, setting healthier boundaries, and prioritizing self-care. The transformative power of these strategies became evident as they not only alleviated my own anxiety but also improved my ability to navigate social relationships with a new sense of clarity and empathy.

Looking at the broader societal landscape, it became clear that the need for such strategies is more pressing than ever. The pace of life, constant connectivity, and social expectations often contribute to high levels of stress and anxiety. This personal experience underscored the urgency of addressing anxiety on both an individual and collective level.

In this chapter, we will explore strategies that not only serve as personal coping mechanisms but also contribute to reshaping the broader narrative about well-being in our society. From this moment on, and approaching the end of the book, the premise is to commit to this knowledge and experience. In this way, we aim to inspire a collective shift towards a more conscious and caring approach to life, one that recognizes the importance of mental well-being in the fabric of our interconnected social existence.

Mindfulness: Cultivating Presence in the Present Moment

In the realm of managing anxiety and cultivating a transformative daily life experience, mindfulness stands out as a powerful and empowering practice. At its core, mindfulness involves intentionally directing one's attention to the present moment, free from judgment or preconceived notions. By nurturing a heightened awareness of thoughts, feelings, and bodily sensations, individuals can carve out a mental space that facilitates a more balanced and deliberate response to the challenges of daily existence.

What makes mindfulness particularly impactful is its versatility—it transcends being merely a meditative exercise and evolves into a way of being that seamlessly integrates into various aspects of daily activities. It's a dynamic practice that extends beyond formal meditation sessions, encouraging individuals to infuse moments of mindfulness into the fabric of their everyday lives.

Whether it's savoring the intricate flavors of a meal, engaging in a mindful walk that attunes one to the sensations of each step, or simply pausing to take a few conscious breaths amidst the chaos of a hectic day, these intentional moments of presence hold the potential to significantly contribute to a calmer, more centered approach to life.

In the hustle and bustle of modern living, mindfulness acts as a gentle anchor, providing individuals with a refuge from the constant stream of thoughts and stressors. It is a reminder that, amidst life's complexities, there is value in grounding oneself in the richness of the present moment. This practice allows for a conscious acknowledgment of emotions, thoughts, and surroundings, paving the way for a more nuanced and compassionate engagement with both oneself and the external world.

As individuals embrace mindfulness as an integral aspect of their daily routine, they embark on a journey towards not only managing anxiety but also enhancing their overall well-being. The transformative power of mindfulness lies in its ability to foster a profound shift in perspective, encouraging individuals to approach challenges with greater resilience, acceptance, and a genuine appreciation for the intricate tapestry of their lives.

Relaxation Techniques

These techniques, spanning a spectrum of practices, offer a holistic approach to alleviating stress and fostering a greater sense of well-being. Among the diverse array of relaxation techniques, three stand out prominently: deep breathing exercises, progressive muscle relaxation, and guided imagery.

Deep breathing exercises emerge as a simple yet powerful tool to signal the body's relaxation response and soothe the nervous system. This intentional focus on breath can be seamlessly woven into daily routines, offering moments of tranquility amid the hustle and bustle.

Progressive muscle relaxation provides another avenue for releasing accumulated tension. This technique involves a systematic process of tensing and then releasing different muscle groups throughout the body. Incorporating progressive muscle relaxation into your routine fosters heightened body awareness and an increased ability to unwind even during demanding moments.

Guided imagery serves as a particularly immersive relaxation practice, allowing individuals to mentally transport themselves to serene and tranquil landscapes. By vividly envisioning calming scenes or scenarios, individuals can detach from the stresses of daily life, promoting a deep sense of relaxation.

Transforming Your Daily Life: Integrating Mindfulness and Relaxation

The seamless fusion of mindfulness and relaxation techniques emerges as a transformative force, reshaping the very fabric of our daily existence. The synergy between these two practices forms a harmonious alliance, offering individuals a holistic approach to confront the multifaceted challenges that life presents. This alliance is not merely a compilation of exercises but a profound shift in perspective, a conscious decision to engage with each moment in a way that fosters both mental clarity and emotional equilibrium.

Imagine awakening each morning to the gentle embrace of a brief mindfulness meditation—a deliberate act that not only anchors you in the present but also sets a positive and intentional tone for the day ahead. As the day unfolds, pockets of mindful breathing become like islands of tranquility amidst the tumultuous waves of responsibilities and demands. In these moments, individuals find composure and resilience, tapping into the deep well of inner calm that is cultivated through the practice of mindfulness.

As the day draws to a close, the intentional integration continues with a guided relaxation exercise—a soothing balm for the accumulated stresses and strains. This deliberate unwinding is not just a prelude to sleep but a ritual that acknowledges the need for restoration. It becomes a bridge between the demanding pace of the day and the serene stillness of the night, paving the way for restful sleep and rejuvenation.

This intentional integration of mindfulness and relaxation techniques is a pathway to empowerment. It is a conscious choice to engage with life on a deeper level, recognizing that the quality of our moments defines the quality of our lives. In fostering a mindset of resilience, individuals not only manage anxiety but also elevate their overall well-being. The transformation unfolds not in grand gestures but in the subtle art of being present, breathing deeply, and intentionally embracing the ebb and flow of life's complexities. Through this intentional practice, individuals forge a sustainable foundation that resonates with the rhythm of a balanced and fulfilling existence.

Music and Anxiety Reduction

The relationship between music and anxiety reduction is a fascinating and well-explored field, shedding light on the therapeutic potential of music in promoting mental well-being. Beyond the immediate emotional responses, the physiological and psychological impact of music on anxiety is multifaceted and continues to be a subject of active research.

One significant aspect of music's influence on anxiety lies in its ability to modulate the autonomic nervous system. Slow and calming music has been shown to trigger the parasympathetic nervous system, which is responsible for promoting relaxation and reducing the fight-or-flight response associated with anxiety. The rhythmic patterns and tonal qualities of certain genres create a sensory experience that resonates with the body, fostering a sense of tranquility.

Classical music, renowned for its intricate compositions and emotional depth, often features prominently in anxiety reduction strategies. The works of composers like Mozart and Beethoven are frequently recommended for their ability to evoke a range of emotions and stimulate cognitive processes, potentially diverting the mind from anxious thoughts.

Ambient music, characterized by its atmospheric and immersive qualities, offers a different approach. Its minimalistic structures and ethereal soundscapes create a sonic environment that can help individuals escape the pressures of daily life, offering a reprieve from stressors.

Nature sounds, including flowing water, bird songs, or rustling leaves, tap into the concept of biophilia, suggesting that humans have an inherent connection to nature. Listening to these sounds can evoke a sense of calm and connection, providing a mental escape and promoting relaxation.

The phenomenon of binaural beats introduces a unique dimension to anxiety reduction through auditory stimulation. By manipulating brainwave frequencies, proponents argue that specific binaural beat frequencies can induce altered states of consciousness, facilitating relaxation and stress reduction. However, more research is needed to fully understand the mechanisms behind this phenomenon and its efficacy.

It is essential to recognize the subjective nature of musical preferences and responses to different genres. Cultural background, personal experiences, and emotional states significantly influence how individuals perceive and react to music. Therefore, tailoring music choices to individual preferences becomes crucial in optimizing the anxiety-reducing effects of music therapy.

While music can be a valuable complement to anxiety management strategies, it is not a substitute for professional mental health advice and treatment. Consulting mental health professionals for personalized advice and incorporating music as part of a holistic approach to well-being is encouraged. As our understanding of the intricate interplay between music and anxiety deepens, so too does the potential for innovative and effective therapeutic applications.

Healthy Life Choices

Adopting a healthy lifestyle is a holistic approach that can significantly contribute to reducing anxiety. Incorporating various practices that address physical, mental, and emotional well-being can create a foundation for resilience and stress management. Here are several healthy lifestyle choices that may help alleviate anxiety:

Regular Exercise

Engaging in regular physical activity is proven to reduce anxiety by promoting the release of endorphins, the body's natural mood lifters. Activities like walking, jogging, yoga, or strength training can not only improve physical health but also enhance mental well-being.

Balanced Nutrition

A well-balanced diet rich in nutrients supports overall health, including brain function. Foods containing omega-3 fatty acids, antioxidants, and vitamins and minerals can positively impact mood and reduce anxiety. Limiting caffeine and sugar intake can also contribute to more stable energy levels.

Limiting Stressors

Identifying and managing stressors is crucial for anxiety reduction. Learning effective time management, setting realistic goals, and establishing boundaries can help prevent overwhelming feelings and promote a more balanced lifestyle.

Hobbies and Leisure Activities

Engaging in activities that bring joy and relaxation is vital for mental health. Hobbies, whether creative, recreational, or educational, offer a positive outlet for stress and anxiety, allowing individuals to unwind and recharge.

Limiting Substance Use

Avoiding excessive alcohol, nicotine, and other substance use is essential for mental health. These substances can exacerbate anxiety symptoms and disrupt the body's natural stress response.

Therapeutic Techniques

Consider incorporating therapeutic techniques such as cognitive behavioral therapy (CBT) or counseling. These approaches provide tools and coping strategies to manage anxious thoughts and behaviors effectively.

Regular Health Check-ups

Physical health is interconnected with mental well-being. Regular medical check-ups can ensure that any underlying health issues are addressed promptly, preventing them from contributing to anxiety.

Remember that everyone is unique, and finding the combination of lifestyle choices that works best for an individual may take some experimentation. It's also crucial to consult with healthcare professionals, such as therapists or doctors, for personalized guidance and support in managing anxiety.

Establishing a Sleep Routine

Sleep, a fundamental aspect of our well-being, is often compromised in people suffering from anxiety disorders. The intertwined relationship between anxiety and disturbed sleep patterns requires establishing a structured sleep routine. This routine not only addresses immediate sleep-related concerns but also contributes significantly to overall mental health.

Consistency is key when it comes to sleeping, especially for those who suffer from anxiety disorders. Establishing a regular sleep schedule, where the goal is to go to bed and wake up at the same time every day, is a powerful tool. This constant rhythm helps regulate the body's internal clock, promoting a more predictable sleep-wake cycle.

In addition to a consistent sleep schedule, incorporating a relaxing bedtime routine is beneficial for people with anxiety. Engaging in activities that promote relaxation, such as reading a book, practicing gentle yoga, or listening to relaxing music, signals to the body that it is time to relax. These rituals can be essential to mitigate the high state of anxiety that is often experienced at the end of the day.

The impact of technology on sleep cannot be underestimated. The blue light emitted by electronic devices alters the production of melatonin, the sleep hormone. To counteract this, it is essential to limit screen time for at least an hour before bedtime. Creating a screen-free zone allows the mind to disconnect from the stressors of the day and facilitates a smoother transition into a restful state.

Creating a comfortable sleeping environment further contributes to the effectiveness of a sleep routine. A cool, dark, and quiet bedroom, along with a comfortable mattress and pillows, improves sleep quality. These elements create an environment conducive to relaxation, helping to counteract the physical manifestations of anxiety.

Mindfulness and relaxation techniques play a crucial role in managing anxiety before bed. Incorporating deep breathing exercises, progressive muscle relaxation, or guided imagery into your pre-sleep routine helps calm the mind.

It is equally important to be aware of stimulants that can hinder your ability to relax. Caffeine and nicotine, commonly found in beverages and substances, should be avoided in the hours before bedtime. These stimulants can exacerbate anxiety and impede the natural progression toward a state of restful sleep.

Physical activity during the day has been shown to have a positive impact on sleep quality and reduce anxiety levels. Regular exercise, integrated into your daily routine, serves as a natural stress reliever. However, vigorous exercise should be avoided close to bedtime to avoid an increase in arousal levels.

For those experiencing persistent anxiety-related sleep disorders, seeking professional help is a prudent step. Mental health professionals can offer personalized counseling, therapeutic interventions, or medications to address the root causes of anxiety. Addressing underlying issues ensures a more holistic approach to managing anxiety and its impact on sleep. Beyond addressing immediate sleep issues, a structured routine contributes significantly to overall mental well-being.

The Deep Relationship Between Sleep and Mental Health

The interaction between mental health and sleep is a complex and dynamic relationship that significantly influences an individual's overall well-being. This intricate relationship involves a constant back-and-forth interaction, where mental health can affect sleep and, conversely, sleep quality can affect mental state. One thing leads to another, in the sense that if we sleep well, we promote a better mindset to take care of our mental health, and by taking care of our mental health, we will have a better chance of having an excellent night's sleep.

Mental health disorders, such as anxiety and depression, often overshadow the ability to achieve restful sleep. The incessant whirlwind of thoughts, worries, and stress that characterizes these conditions can make it difficult to relax and enter a state of relaxation conducive to sleep. As a result, people with mental health problems may experience difficulty falling asleep, staying asleep, or enjoying the full regenerative benefits of sleep.

The ebb and flow of brain activity throughout the various stages of sleep is a critical component of the sleep cycle. These stages contribute to overall brain health by orchestrating fluctuations in activity in different brain regions and ultimately improving cognitive functions such as thinking, learning, and memory. Recent research has shed light on the profound impact of sleep-induced brain activity on emotional and mental well-being.

While we sleep, the brain is involved in the evaluation and retention of thoughts and memories, with a notable emphasis on the consolidation of positive emotional content. In particular, lack of sleep or lack of REM sleep can negatively affect this process, influencing mood and emotional responsiveness and, most importantly, contributing to the development of sleep disorders (Suni & Dimitriu, 2023).

Sleep is not simply a passive state; rather, it is a dynamic process that contributes to cognitive functioning, emotional regulation, and stress resilience. Inadequate or disrupted sleep can exacerbate existing mental health problems and contribute to the development of new challenges, creating a cyclical pattern that can be difficult to break.

The impact of sleep on mental health extends beyond common conditions like anxiety and depression. Research has shown that chronic sleep deprivation is associated with an increased risk of developing psychiatric disorders, including bipolar disorder and schizophrenia. Additionally, people with sleep disorders, such as insomnia or sleep apnea, often report elevated levels of stress, anxiety, and depression.

Understanding and addressing this reciprocal relationship is essential to promoting holistic well-being. Interventions targeting both mental health and sleep can break the cycle and contribute to overall improvement.

Additionally, taking a comprehensive approach to mental health that includes sleep hygiene practices can lead to positive results. Establishing a consistent sleep routine, creating a comfortable sleeping environment, and incorporating relaxation techniques are crucial steps in promoting better sleep, which, in turn, supports mental health.

On the other hand, strategies aimed at improving mental health can have a positive impact on sleep. Therapeutic interventions, stress reduction techniques, and mindfulness practices have been shown to improve sleep quality. By addressing the root causes of mental health problems, people can pave the way for more restorative and rejuvenating sleep experiences.

Sleep and Anxiety Disorders

Each year, approximately 20% of adults in the United States face anxiety disorders. Furthermore, around 25% of adolescents are affected by these disorders. Anxiety disorders, which encompass conditions such as general anxiety disorder, social anxiety disorder, panic disorder, specific phobias, obsessive-compulsive disorder (OCD), and post-traumatic stress disorder (PTSD), manifest as excessive fear or worry, significantly affecting daily life and posing risks for health problems such as heart disease and diabetes (Suri & Dimitriu, 2023).

The correlation between anxiety disorders and sleep problems is notable. The elevated levels of worry and fear associated with anxiety contribute to a state of hyperarousal characterized by a racing mind. This hyperarousal is recognized as a central factor contributing to insomnia. Consequently, sleep-related problems can become an additional source of worry, leading to anticipatory anxiety at bedtime, making it difficult to initiate sleep.

Studies have established a particularly strong link between PTSD and sleep disorders. People with PTSD often engage in replaying negative events in their minds, encounter nightmares, and experience increased alertness, all of which can disrupt normal sleep patterns. This is particularly relevant for veterans, as at least 90% of U.S. veterans with combat-related post-traumatic stress disorder from recent wars report symptoms of insomnia (Suri & Dimitriu, 2023).

The Role of Therapy in the Management of Anxiety

Therapy plays a critical role in the effective management of anxiety, offering people a structured and supportive environment to explore and address the challenges associated with their anxiety disorders. Whether it is generalized anxiety disorder, social anxiety disorder, panic disorder, specific phobias, OCD, or PTSD, therapy provides valuable tools and strategies to navigate the complex terrain of anxious thoughts and emotions.

One of the main modalities used in the management of anxiety is cognitive behavioral therapy (CBT). CBT aims to identify and modify negative thought patterns and behaviors that contribute to anxiety. Through collaborative efforts between the individual and the therapist, CBT helps reshape distorted thinking and cultivate healthy responses to stressors. By fostering awareness and understanding of triggers, people can learn adaptive coping mechanisms and gradually gain mastery over their anxiety.

Exposure therapy is another effective therapeutic approach, particularly beneficial for specific phobias and post-traumatic stress disorder. This method involves gradual and systematic exposure to feared stimuli or situations in a controlled and supportive environment. Over time, repeated exposure helps desensitize people to their anxieties, decreasing the intensity of their emotional reactions and promoting a sense of mastery and control.

Mindfulness-based therapies, such as mindfulness-based stress reduction (MBSR) and acceptance and commitment therapy (ACT), are gaining importance in anxiety management. These approaches emphasize being present in the moment, recognizing thoughts and feelings without judgment, and encouraging non-reactive awareness. People can develop a more adaptive relationship with their anxiety, reducing its impact on their overall well-being.

Interpersonal therapy (IPT) is particularly useful in addressing social anxiety disorder as it focuses on improving interpersonal relationships and communication skills. IPT helps people identify and navigate interaction patterns that contribute to anxiety, promoting healthier ways of connecting with others.

In addition to these evidence-based therapeutic approaches, the therapeutic alliance itself plays a crucial role in anxiety management. The supportive relationship between the individual and the therapist provides a safe space for exploration, validation, and the development of coping mechanisms. The therapist acts as a guide and offers knowledge, encouragement, and personalized strategies tailored to the individual's specific challenges.

Additionally, therapy provides a platform for people to explore the root causes of their anxiety, often uncovering underlying issues that contribute to their emotional distress. This deeper understanding allows people to address not only the symptoms but also the core issues driving their anxiety, fostering long-term resilience.

The collaborative nature of the therapy, combined with its focus on self-discovery and skill development, makes it an invaluable resource for those seeking effective, long-lasting relief from anxiety. Through evidence-based modalities, the therapeutic process empowers individuals to confront and overcome their anxiety, equipping them with the tools and knowledge necessary for sustained well-being.

In concluding the insightful exploration within the chapter "Wellness in Anxiety," it becomes evident that a holistic approach to well-being is intricately linked to the effective management of anxiety disorders. By delving into the realms of healthy eating habits, the promotion of restful sleep, and the nurturing of mental health, we have uncovered a comprehensive set of strategies vital for navigating and ultimately overcoming the intricate challenges associated with anxiety.

As our focus shifts toward the forthcoming and final chapter of this dedicated volume on anxiety, titled "Positive Changes for a Fulfilling Social Life," we find ourselves on the threshold of the culminating phase of this captivating journey. This chapter promises to be a beacon of guidance, steering us toward profound insights into the transformative power of trusting the process. Beyond this, it encourages the cultivation of a robust social and familial support network, underlining the profound impact that meaningful relationships can have on one's journey toward a fulfilled and satisfying life.

In the upcoming pages, we are poised to explore the essence of positive change not only as an individual pursuit but also as a catalyst for inspiring others to enhance their own lives. The exploration of the intricate dynamics of human connections will take center stage, illuminating the pivotal role that constructive and meaningful relationships play in the pursuit of a well-rounded and contented existence.

As we traverse the narratives and lessons encapsulated within "Positive Changes for a Fulfilling Social Life," we will gain a deeper understanding of the interconnectedness of personal growth, social bonds, and the overall fabric of well-being. Through this collective effort, we envisage a community enriched by mutual support, shared aspirations, and a collective commitment to inspire positive changes for a brighter and more fulfilling future.

Chapter 8:

Positive Changes for a Fulfilling Social Life

Embarking on a journey to overcome anxiety disorders is a brave step towards building a more fulfilling social life. Positive changes in various aspects of life play a fundamental role in this transformative process. No journey is meant to be taken alone. Sharing your experiences and challenges with those who understand and care can bring you immense relief. Open communication fosters deeper connections, making your social interactions more meaningful and positive.

As you walk the path of self-discovery and resilience, embracing these changes can lead to a richer, more fulfilling social existence. The first step towards a fulfilling social life is to take the time to understand your thoughts and emotions, recognizing patterns that trigger anxiety. It is about understanding the triggering factors of this condition and thus being able to respond more effectively in social situations.

A fulfilling social life is closely linked to your overall well-being. To deepen and strengthen these aspects, we must understand that self-care practices are regular exercises in our daily routine. This contributes to a more resilient mindset and better social interactions.

Anxiety often arises from negative self-talk and distorted perceptions. The positive changes outlined in this book mean challenging these thoughts by replacing them with more rational and positive affirmations.

In this final chapter, think about accepting positive changes as part of the path. You're looking to overcome anxiety disorders, which is a dynamic and complex process, but it'll lead to a fuller social life.

Reflecting on Progress

Reflecting on personal growth involves not only recognizing the external changes in your behavior but also appreciating the internal changes in your thinking. Consider times when you were faced with anxiety-provoking situations and responded differently than before. Maybe you managed to stay present and grounded, practiced deep breathing, or challenged negative thoughts. Recognize these instances as evidence of your evolving coping mechanisms and emotional resilience.

Much of what it means to deal with anxiety has to do with the ability to be introspective when analyzing what is happening around us and with us. Personally, this ability to look inward and find the positives and negatives helped me along the way. As we mentioned at the beginning of the book, anxiety is a feeling that is practically impossible to "eliminate." It is not something that we can eradicate from our minds, but rather, we must learn to live with it. We must learn to find the right balance so that it does not negatively affect our lives. If, regardless of what we do, anxiety will be there, then let it be to add value to our existence.

Furthermore, personal growth goes beyond mere survival; it encompasses thriving in the face of adversity. Take note of newfound strengths, such as greater empathy, greater self-awareness, and a deeper understanding of your emotional triggers. Embracing these aspects of personal growth not only builds confidence but also reinforces the idea that challenges can be transformative opportunities. It is about recognizing, adopting, incorporating, and strengthening a positive mindset that always drives us forward. Positivity is a transformative force that constantly invites us to progress, and progress brings evolution.

Cultivate a Positive Mindset

Mindset is largely defined as the emotional reaction to common daily routines, playing a crucial role in health and quality of life. Although you may not have the power to change significant aspects such as your job, family, or place of residence, which could be sources of negative thoughts, you can face daily frustrations with a positive attitude. This is achieved by questioning those negative thoughts and improving your perspective on life (Keng et al., 2011).

Cultivating a positive mindset involves consciously directing your thoughts toward optimism and hope. Challenge automatic negative thoughts that may arise during times of anxiety. Instead, actively look for the positive aspects of situations and focus on your strengths. A positive mindset is not about denying challenges; rather, it is about presenting them as manageable and surmountable.

Focusing on positive thinking does not mean ignoring the less pleasant situations that life can present. Rather, it means facing the unpleasant in a more optimistic and constructive way, believing in the best rather than anticipating the worst.

The basis of positive thinking is usually found in self-talk, that constant stream of unexpressed thoughts passing through the mind. These automatic thoughts can vary between positive and negative. Some of these come from logic and reason, while others may originate from misconceptions generated by a lack of information or expectations based on preconceived concepts of what could happen.

If most of the thoughts that arise in your mind tend to be negative, you probably have a more pessimistic outlook on life. On the other hand, if your thoughts are primarily positive, you are likely an optimist, someone who practices positive thinking (Mayo Clinic, 2023).

As we mentioned above, integrating daily practices like mindfulness meditation or gratitude exercises further reinforces a positive mindset. These activities help anchor your thoughts in the present moment, fostering appreciation for the positive aspects of your life. Over time, a positive mindset becomes a powerful ally, influencing your perception of challenges and shaping your response to them.

Conscious Reflection

Mindful reflection is a nuanced process that involves observing your thoughts and emotions without judgment. Spend time introspecting and create a safe space for self-exploration. As you reflect, consider the patterns of your anxiety triggers and corresponding emotional responses. Mindful reflection facilitates a deeper understanding of your internal landscape, allowing you to make informed decisions about your coping strategies and areas for improvement.

This kind of thinking involves a strategic approach to goal setting. Make sure your goals are specific, measurable, attainable, relevant, and time-bound (SMART). Breaking down larger goals into smaller, manageable steps not only clarifies the path forward but also provides a sense of accomplishment at each stage.

Fostering a growth mindset means accepting challenges as opportunities for learning and development. Recognize that your abilities and intelligence are not fixed but can be cultivated through dedication and effort. This shift in mindset views anxiety-provoking situations as opportunities to acquire new skills, deepen self-understanding, and improve coping mechanisms. As you foster a growth mindset, you will feel more resilient in the face of challenges, actively seek opportunities for personal development, and embrace the transformative nature of the journey.

Reflecting on progress, recognizing personal growth, and cultivating a positive mindset form a holistic approach to overcoming anxiety. This ongoing process of self-discovery and positive transformation becomes a ray of hope that guides you toward a future characterized by personal empowerment and emotional well-being.

Building a Supportive and Positive Social Network

The importance of a positive and supportive social network cannot be underestimated. Our connections with others play a critical role in shaping our experiences, influencing our emotional well-being, and contributing to our overall quality of life. This section explores the importance of building a strong social network and offers ideas for cultivating relationships that foster positivity and support.

At the center of a fulfilled life is the foundation of positive social interactions. Humans are inherently social creatures, and our relationships impact various facets of our lives, from mental and emotional health to physical well-being. A supportive social network provides a safety net in times of adversity and magnifies the joy of life's triumphs.

Building a social support network involves fostering connections that go beyond mere knowledge. True support is based on empathy, active listening, and genuine concern for the well-being of others. It's about creating a space where people feel comfortable expressing their vulnerabilities, knowing that they will be received with understanding and encouragement.

Diversity and inclusion are essential elements of a positive social network. Connecting with people of diverse backgrounds, experiences, and perspectives enriches our lives, expands our understanding, and fosters a sense of belonging. Embracing diversity within our social circles contributes to a more vibrant and resilient community.

While diversity is crucial, shared values and interests create bonds that strengthen social connections. Aligning with people who share similar passions or principles provides a foundation for deeper understanding and shared experiences. This shared foundation often acts as a catalyst for positive collaboration and mutual growth.

Reciprocity forms the backbone of a positive social network. Establishing trust and a dynamic of give and take strengthens relationships. Knowing that support is a two-way street fosters a sense of trustworthiness and deepens the ties within the network. Trust serves as an adhesive that unites people, creating a resilient and lasting social fabric.

Effective communication is the cornerstone of positive relationships. Open, honest, and respectful communication builds trust and understanding. It allows people within the network to express their needs, share their experiences, and navigate conflicts constructively.

Positive communication fosters an environment where everyone feels heard and valued.

A supportive social network contributes to emotional resilience, helping people face life's challenges with greater strength and adaptability. Knowing that there is a network of supportive people provides a sense of security, making it easier to face adversity and recover from setbacks.

Intentionally cultivating positivity within the social network helps create an uplifting atmosphere. Celebrating achievements, expressing gratitude, and focusing on the positive aspects of life collectively create an environment that fosters well-being. Shared moments of joy become the pillars of a positive and resilient community.

In reflecting on my personal journey, I vividly recall the profound impact of intentionally nurturing a support network. Actively engaging in community events and approaching interactions with genuine empathy and openness allowed me to form connections that went beyond mere surface-level encounters.

A few years ago, I faced the challenge of reengaging with people, driven by the overwhelming nature of discussions amidst the pandemic and evolving political climate. Interacting with certain individuals began to heighten my anxiety, prompting me to withdraw and find solace in the comfort of my home. Recognizing the toll of isolation on my well-being, I made a conscious effort to reconnect with others. Setting boundaries became essential, and I started informing visitors in advance about topics that were better left untouched to ensure our interactions remained positive.

These steps in building a positive social network extend far beyond individual lives, contributing to a collective narrative of shared growth, joy, and mutual support. It's a journey marked by understanding, resilience, and the power of fostering meaningful connections.

You'll see that the steps taken to build a positive social network resonate far beyond individual lives, shaping a collective narrative of shared growth, joy, and support.

Maintaining Momentum in Time

Navigating anxiety is not a sprint but a marathon that requires sustained effort and commitment over time. Anxiety, as we mentioned, is a constant presence. Understanding that this psychological companion is likely to persist underscores the importance of maintaining momentum in managing its impact on our lives.

Anxiety, in its various forms, tends to be a persistent force woven into the fabric of daily existence. Accepting this reality is the first step toward developing a sustainable strategy to maintain control. Unlike a fleeting storm, anxiety lingers on the horizon, sometimes just a gentle drizzle and other times a torrential downpour. Recognizing that it is an ongoing process allows people to adopt a proactive and empowering mindset.

The nature of anxiety means that efforts to control it should not be sporadic but rather a continuous and intentional effort. It requires a commitment to self-awareness and a proactive approach to maintaining mental well-being. Just as we engage in daily rituals to care for our physical health, the same diligence should be applied to our mental health.

Developing coping mechanisms that align with the ebb and flow of anxiety takes time and perseverance. It's about creating a repertoire of strategies that work for you and integrating them seamlessly into your daily life. These strategies may include mindfulness practices, positive affirmations, or structured routines that provide stability amid the unpredictable nature of anxiety.

Consistency is the linchpin of the effort to maintain momentum. Establishing a routine that incorporates activities that promote mental well-being, even during periods of relative calm, can strengthen your resilience when anxiety escalates. It's a proactive stance that serves as an ongoing investment in your mental health, similar to tending a garden regularly to ensure it flourishes.

The metaphor of maintaining momentum also implies an understanding of the cyclical nature of anxiety. There will be peaks and valleys, moments of intense unrest interspersed with periods of relative calm. This recognition allows individuals to navigate the undulating terrain of their mental landscape with a steadiness that comes from experience and self-awareness.

Below, I will give you three tips to learn to be constant in life and be able to maintain in the best possible way all the effort and energy that you have given to this proposal of controlling anxiety:

Create positive routines and habits: Consistency is strengthened by incorporating positive routines and habits into your daily life. Establish a structure that includes moments dedicated to your goals. Consistency in these activities will gradually build the discipline necessary to maintain momentum over time.

Cultivate resilience: Consistency often requires a healthy dose of self-motivation. Resilience is essential. Understand that you will face setbacks and obstacles, but the ability to recover and continue is what will allow you to remain consistent over time.

Maintain a positive focus and visualize success: Visualize success, imagining how you will feel when you achieve your goals. This practice not only strengthens your motivation but also helps you get through difficult times.

Inspiring Others on Their Journey

Inspiring others on their journey is a profound and rewarding endeavor that involves sharing experiences, wisdom, and encouragement to uplift and motivate those walking their own paths. Whether on a personal or professional journey, the ability to inspire others can have a positive effect, fostering resilience, growth, and positivity. Here are several things to consider when it comes to inspiring others on their journey.

Part of inspiring others has to do with being authentic. Share your journey honestly, embracing both successes and challenges. Vulnerability creates a relatable connection, allowing others to see that the path to growth is often filled with ups and downs.

Demonstrate the values and principles you uphold through your own actions. Setting an example means embodying the qualities you want to inspire in others. Whether it's resilience, perseverance, or a positive mindset, your consistent behavior serves as a powerful model for those seeking to navigate their trajectories with similar attributes.

Inspiring others requires a genuine understanding of their unique challenges and aspirations. Practice active listening to truly understand their experiences. Empathy allows you to connect emotionally, creating a supportive environment where people feel seen and understood.

Positivity has a great impact on inspiration. Offer genuine words of encouragement to build their confidence and motivation. Additionally, provide constructive feedback focused on growth and improvement rather than criticism. Constructive guidance helps people see challenges as development opportunities rather than insurmountable obstacles.

Narratives have a profound impact on motivation. Share inspiring stories, whether yours or those of individuals who have overcome adversity. Personal anecdotes can serve as beacons of hope, illustrating that challenges can be overcome and transformation is possible. The real-life stories resonate deeply and provide tangible examples of resilience and success.

Guide people to set realistic but ambitious goals. Encourage them to imagine the future they want and the steps necessary to achieve it. Assisting in creating a clear vision provides direction and purpose, fueling the determination needed for the path ahead. Regularly review and celebrate progress toward these goals to maintain motivation.

Inspiring others on their journey is a transformative act that involves authenticity, empathy, and a commitment to positive influence. By sharing your experiences, leading by example, and providing support, you contribute to the collective empowerment of those who navigate your paths. Remember that the impact of inspiration extends far beyond the individual and has the potential to shape a community of resilient, motivated, and fulfilled people.

Conclusion

At the culmination of this exhaustive exploration of anxiety disorders, the imperative need is not to perceive anxiety as a personal weakness but rather as a natural affliction that, while may be limiting, does not define the essence of one's life. The key is to put ourselves in the situation of those who experience it. The importance of maintaining a positive mindset in daily life and learning to coexist with inevitable feelings of anxiety stands as a fundamental pillar for a full and meaningful existence.

Living day-to-day with anxiety disorders presents a series of challenges that, for those who experience it, can resemble navigating turbulent waters. With its ability to color everyday experiences with constant worry and internal tensions, anxiety can become an overwhelming challenge that affects not only mental health but also overall quality of life.

In this complex scenario, the techniques and strategies presented in this book stand as beacons of hope and practical tools to overcome these challenges. The central idea is to not only cope with anxiety but to conquer the terrain of these difficult sensations. This process of overcoming anxiety does not involve completely eliminating anxiety since it is a natural emotion, but rather learning to manage it in a healthier and more constructive way.

The techniques explored in these pages not only provide a set of tools for coping with anxiety, but also offer a path to self-discovery and self-affirmation. Rather than allowing anxiety to dictate the pace of daily life, these strategies seek to empower those who apply them, giving them control over their emotional responses and behaviors.

The process of overcoming oneself in the context of anxiety involves not only understanding the roots of these emotional challenges but also developing the resilience necessary to confront them. Conquering this difficult terrain means accepting that each small step forward, each application of a learned technique, constitutes a significant triumph on the path to a more balanced and fulfilling life.

Throughout the pages of this book, the different facets of anxiety have been explored in detail. From its intricate impact on family dynamics to its influence on the most significant relationships, through its imprint on the professional sphere and its penetration into the deepest aspects of life, each chapter has woven a comprehensive narrative about how anxiety can intertwine in the daily fabric of our human interactions.

Overcoming difficulties is not about completely eliminating difficulties but about learning to live with them in a way that does not restrict personal fulfillment or meaningful connections. It is about adopting these strategies so that those living with anxiety disorders have the possibility of writing a new and more strengthening chapter in their story, where personal conquest becomes the main narrative.

The challenges associated with anxiety disorders are intensified in the context of modernity, where today's society often demands more than many individuals can offer. This contemporary environment is characterized by an accelerated speed of change, constant interconnection through technology, and increasing expectations in various aspects of life.

One of the crucial challenges is the constant pressure to always be connected and available. Technology, although it has provided significant benefits, has generated a culture of permanent availability. Work, social, and family demands can converge in a continuous flow, leaving little room for rest and recovery.

The constant search for success and comparison through social media also generates an additional level of stress. Contemporary society, with its focus on visibility and performance, can induce a constant feeling of inadequacy. Expectations related to career success, perfect relationships, and idealized beauty standards can be overwhelming.

Furthermore, the speed of modern life often leaves little time for reflection and meaningful personal connections. Constant overstimulation and multitasking can deplete mental and emotional resources, contributing to feelings of being overwhelmed and lacking time for self-care.

In this context, people facing anxiety disorders are often expected to respond to these challenges with exceptional resilience and adaptability. However, it is essential to recognize that everyone has limits and that constant overexertion can have significant impacts on mental health.

Addressing these challenges requires a cultural shift and a reassessment of societal priorities. It is essential to encourage empathy and mutual support, as well as recognize the importance of establishing healthy boundaries. Society can benefit from promoting a more balanced approach that values mental health as much as external achievements, allowing people to live full and meaningful lives without feeling constantly burdened by the overwhelming expectations of the modern era.

The journey outlined in these pages boils down to the ability to understand anxiety and, just as important, to develop practical strategies to build stronger, richer interpersonal connections. A call to action resonates in the conclusion, urging readers to apply the valuable lessons learned in their daily lives and to offer ongoing support to those facing anxiety-related challenges.

The conclusion stands as a vital reminder that anxiety should not be the defining force of people or their relationships. This book provides knowledge but also establishes itself as a reliable guide on the path to more conscious and healthy human interaction. Underscoring that understanding, empathy, and mutual support are powerful tools in the management of anxiety, the work culminates by reaffirming that the path to continuous improvement is within reach of all those willing to undertake it.

Bonus

As a thank you for choosing this book, I have created A Guide to Managing Anxiety to help you identify your anxiety symptoms and choose self-care practices to manage your anxiety and experience calmness.

Please scan the QR Code or go to the following link to receive the complimentary Guide to Managing Anxiety.

https://tinyurl.com/SHP-Anxiety-Guide

Book Review

Thank you for reading my book. If you enjoyed it and found it insightful, I would sincerely appreciate your review of the book. Reviews are helpful to other readers and authors. QR Codes are provided on the next page that link to some direct marketplaces for submitting a review.

United States

Austrailia

Canada

France

United Kingdom

References

Beck, M. (2011, November 23). *Party on: A survival guide for social-phobes*. Martha Beck. https://marthabeck.com/2011/11/party-on/

Benson, K. (2017, August 23) *Breaking the pursue-withdraw pattern: An interview with Scott R. Woolley, Ph.D.* The Gottman Institute. https://www.gottman.com/blog/breaking-pursue-withdraw-pattern-interview-scott-r-woolley-ph-d/

Bhandari, S. (2023, January 7). *All about anxiety disorders: From causes to treatment and prevention.* WebMD. https://www.webmd.com/anxiety-panic/anxiety-disorders

Catalunya, U. O. de. (n.d.). *El sindrome del impostor: el 70% de los trabajadores cree no merecer su exito profesional.* [*The impostor syndrome: 70% of workers believe they do not deserve their professional success.*] UOC (Universitat Oberta de Catalunya). https://www.uoc.edu/portal/es/news/actualitat/2019/172-sindrome-impostor.html

CEPFAMI. (2024). *Home.* Cepfami. https://cepfami.com/

Cherry, K. (2022, February 21). *How to know if you are in a healthy relationship.* Verywell Mind. https://www.verywellmind.com/all-about-healthy-relationship-4774802

"Contras" de enamorarse para quienes sufren trastornos de ansiedad. ["Cons" of falling in love for those suffering from anxiety disorders]. (2017, October 27). Infobae. https://www.infobae.com/2008/05/02/377281-contras-enamorarse-quienes-sufren-trastornos-ansiedad/

Create your own happiness: Cultivate a positive mindset. (2023, February 27). PracticingPositive. https://www.practicingpositive.com/create-your-own-happiness-mindset/

Felman, A. (2023, November 14). *What to know about social anxiety disorder.* MedicalNewsToday. https://www.medicalnewstoday.com/articles/176891

Graded exercise as an approach for mental health. (n.d.). Physiopedia. https://www.physio-pedia.com/Graded_exercise_as_an_approach_for_Mental_health

Greene, L. (2020, August 17). *Proven ways to develop a positive mindset—and why it matters.* Psycom. https://www.psycom.net/positive-thinking

Hailey, L. (n.d.). *How to set boundaries: 5 ways to draw the line politely.* Science of People. https://www.scienceofpeople.com/how-to-set-boundaries/

Healthy lifestyle choices. (2019, February 12). MyClinic. https://myclinicgroup.com.au/healthy-lifestyle-choices/

Keng, S. L., Smoski, M. J., & Robins, C. J. (2011). Effects of Mindfulness on Psychological health: a review of empirical studies. *Clinical Psychology Review, 31*(6), 1041–1056. https://doi.org/10.1016/j.cpr.2011.04.006

Littrell, J. (2008). *The mind-body connection.* Social Work in Health Care, 46(4), 17–37. https://doi.org/10.1300/j010v46n04_02

Madden, T. (2023, February 2). *How to build and maintain professional relationships.* Forbes. https://www.forbes.com/sites/forbescoachescouncil/2023/02/02/how-to-build-and-maintain-professional-relationships/

Mayo Clinic. (2022, February 3). *Positive thinking: Stop negative self-talk to reduce stress*. Mayo Clinic. https://www.mayoclinic.org/healthy-lifestyle/stress-management/in-depth/positive-thinking/art-20043950

MedlinePlus. (2016, November 4). *Anxiety*. Medlineplus.gov. https://medlineplus.gov/anxiety.html#:~:text=Anxiety%20is%20a%20feeling%20of

Morin, A. (2023, December 15). *How to face your fears when you want to tackle them head-on*. Verywell Mind. https://www.verywellmind.com/healthy-ways-to-face-your-fears-4165487

O'Bryan, A. (2022, February 8). *How to practice active listening: 16 examples & techniques*. PositivePsychology. https://positivepsychology.com/active-listening-techniques/

Parvez, H. (2020, November 27) *Assertiveness vs aggressiveness*. PsychMechanics. https://www.psychmechanics.com/assertiveness-vs-aggressiveness/

Pérez, A. H. (2020, October 23). *Qué decirle a una persona con ansiedad [What to say to a person with anxiety]*. Psicólogos Animae. https://psicologosanimae.com/que-decirle-a-una-persona-con-ansiedad/

Raypole, C (2013, March 28) *How to support your romantic partner living with anxiety*. Psych Central. https://psychcentral.com/anxiety/how-to-help-romantic-partner-living-with-anxiety

Sakulku, J., & Alexander, J. (2011). *The impostor phenomenon*. https://www.sciencetheearth.com/uploads/2/4/6/5/24658156/2011_sakulku_the_impostor_phenomenon.pdf

Self reflection, self confidence, self management. (n.d.). Elevate Consulting Group. https://www.elevate-consulting.com/en/self-reflection-self-confidence-self-management/

Stahl, A. (2023, October 9). *3 ways to turn rejection into fuel in your career.* Forbes. https://www.forbes.com/sites/ashleystahl/2023/10/09/3-ways-to-turn-rejection-into-fuel-in-your-career/?sh=44e445f96839

Suni, E., & Dimitriu, A. (2023, November 16). *Mental health and sleep.* Sleep Foundation. https://www.sleepfoundation.org/mental-health

Telch, M. (n.d.). *The nature and causes of anxiety and panic.* https://labs.la.utexas.edu/telch/files/2015/08/Nature-and-Causes-8.10.15.pdf

The Power of Social Connections at Work. (2023, June 29). Strive Well-Being. https://strive2bfit.com/resources/the-power-of-social-connections-at-work/

Vora, T. (2016, June 14) *Journey that inspires others.* QAspire Consulting. https://qaspire.com/journey-that-inspires-others/

Why do people act differently in groups than they do alone? (2019, February 14). Walden University. https://www.waldenu.edu/online-masters-programs/ms-in-psychology/resource/why-do-people-act-differently-in-groups-than-they-do-alone

Why is social wellness important? (2022). University of Nebraska Omaha. Www.unomaha.edu. https://www.unomaha.edu/student-life/presidents-wellness-committee/social-wellness.php

Young, V. (2017, November 28) *10 steps you can use to overcome impostor syndrome.* Impostor Syndrome Institute.

https://impostorsyndrome.com/articles/10-steps-overcome-impostor/

Made in the USA
Thornton, CO
09/21/24 02:21:37